Bond
No.1 for exam success

Non-verbal Reasoning

Assessment Practice for the 11+

Ages 7–8 Year 3

Andrew Baines

OXFORD
UNIVERSITY PRESS

OXFORD
UNIVERSITY PRESS

Great Clarendon Street, Oxford, OX2 6DP, United Kingdom

Oxford University Press is a department of the University of Oxford.
It furthers the University's objective of excellence in research, scholarship, and education by publishing worldwide. Oxford is a registered trade mark of Oxford University Press in the UK and in certain other countries

Written by Andrew Baines with additional material by Alison Primrose

First published in 2025

British Library Cataloguing in Publication Data
Data available

978-1-38-206090-5

10 9 8 7 6 5 4 3 2 1

Printed in China

The manufacturing process conforms to the environmental regulations of the country of origin

MIX
Paper | Supporting responsible forestry
FSC™ C110497
FSC www.fsc.org

Acknowledgements

Content Development Editor and Reviewer: Sue Rowe and Alison Primrose
Page make-up: York Publishing Solutions Pvt. Ltd.
Cover illustrations: Lo Cole
Illustrations: Nigel Kitching and York Publishing Solutions Pvt. Ltd.

Although we have made every effort to trace and contact all copyright holders before publication this has not been possible in all cases. If notified, the publisher will rectify any errors or omissions at the earliest opportunity.

A Brief History of Bond

Bond 11+ has been the market leader in selective school admission test preparation since 1964, when J.M. Bond published her first book of practice tests.

Jean Moyra Bond was a school principal and passionate educator who started writing out practice questions for her pupils on slips of paper, to help get them test-ready, at a time when no formal resources were available. Her high-quality questions spawned a series of books and the Bond range grew from there; however their original author was advised to publish under her initials, rather than her name, as it was felt that the books would not sell as well if it was known they were written by a woman.

Happily, times have changed; but Jean Moyra Bond's legacy lives on, supporting thousands of pupils on their 11+ journey every year. 'J.M.' Bond was involved in writing and revising Bond materials up until her death in 2011, with the baton being passed on to the new generations of expert tutors who create Bond's peerless learning and practice content.

Now offering cutting-edge digital solutions, as well as a comprehensive print range, Bond remains as the gold standard in 11+ preparation to this day.

Contents

Welcome

Bond's non-verbal reasoning resources provide thorough and continuous practice for key non-verbal reasoning skills. They are ideal preparation for the 11+ and other selective school entrance exams.

Bond offers a complete, flexible programme of preparation materials that you can adapt to your child's specific needs. We provide a wide selection of question types and believes that an enriched education is the best preparation. We help children to both master the techniques and develop the logic and rationale to tackle any unknown question types.

KEY STUDY SKILLS

Here are some tips to help:

- **Balance short bursts of practice with longer assessment papers.**
- **Create a quiet study space with pencils, an eraser and paper for working out.**
- **Limit distractions such as television, technology and games.**
- **Remember that errors are useful – they are part of the journey to success.**

A Note for Parents

Parents have a crucial role in helping children and motivating them. Here are some ways that you can really make a difference.

- Check your child is working at the right level. The goal is being able to score 85% on average. It is demotivating if they cannot complete questions.
- Mark work promptly and go through errors. If papers have not been marked, a child has no idea how they are doing or whether they are repeating the same mistakes.
- Limit the range of homework you give your child. The best results are achieved by a system that gradually increases in difficulty. Completing lots of books and papers does not guarantee your child's success and often creates stress.
- If your child is struggling with something specific, add additional support in that area.
- Communication is key. Encourage your child to focus on the positive.

How to Use This Book

It is very important you find the time to work through this book with your child. It is likely they will need support to understand the Key Skill explanations. Once these elements are understood the questions should be more easily accessed by them independently.

This book includes many step-by-step techniques for solving different question types.

- The first section of the book is the Learning Papers that focus on key skills with worked examples then questions for consolidation.
- The second section of the book is Mixed Papers so that children continue to consolidate and do not forget what they have learnt.
- There are fully worked out answers to explain how an answer has been reached.

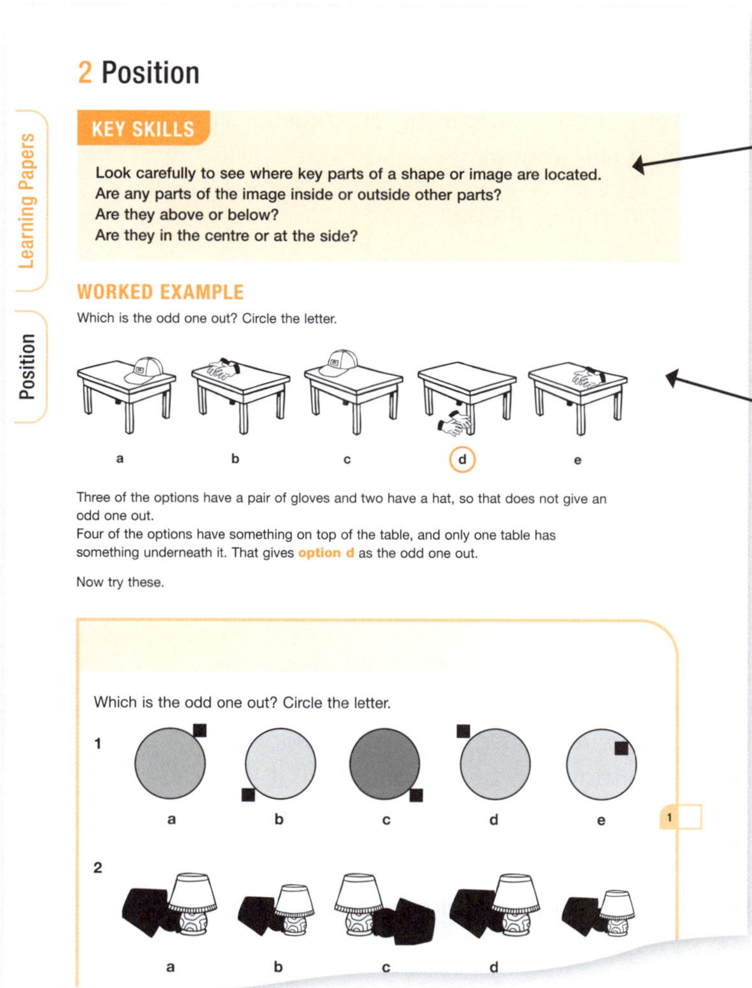

Key Skills highlight the topic then offer tips and strategies to succeed. It is important to read this carefully so that you understand the techniques needed.

Worked Examples offer support so that a child understands what to do and what to look out for. Read this carefully.

The Learning Papers cover key skills in shape connections, codes, completing a shape and spatial reasoning appropriate for children of this age. Bond Assessment Practice draw on a wide variety of skills and question types so that children are always challenged to think and do not get bored of answering same question type repeatedly. These books help children 'think on their feet' and cope with the unexpected.

Do not forget that a rounded education is key. As well as testing skills, the 11+ requires children to possess a wide vocabulary and robust general knowledge.

- Read a range of literature with your child – stories, poems, non-fiction, comics – it all counts.
- Experience new places together such as a visit to a museum or a walk through the woods. New experiences can stimulate interesting discussions, deepen your child's understanding of the world, and help to build essential vocabulary.
- Play games together – card games, board games and sudokus are all excellent ways of developing key skills such as logical reasoning and problem solving and expanding your child's vocabulary.

NON-VERBAL REASONING SKILLS

This Bond 11+ Non-Verbal Reasoning Assessment Practice book is useful for all 11+ exams.The learning papers cover the following key skills:

- **Shape connections** finding a common pattern of shapes, solving analogies, finding the odd shape out, finding a shape most like another.
- **Completing a shape** solving grids, adding or merging shapes.

The Mixed Papers ensure the key skills are consolidated thoroughly. Do not forget that a rounded education is key. Following a diagram to build a Lego model, drawing and colouring in mandala shapes, creating tessellations, making a mosaic with tiles, making friendships bands or woven patterns, completing jigsaw puzzles and playing with STEM toys are all fun ways of developing non-verbal reasoning skills. Hacker Can is a game that teaches computer programming and develops a logical way of thinking.

Each book is part of the Bond system with books increasing gradually in difficulty. Once your child has completed this book, there is a clear progression in starting the next book level if you child has an average score of 85% in this book. If they have achieved an average score of 70%–85%, then another book at this same level will provide further support. If your child has achieved an average score of less than 70%, then moving down a level will be most useful. Once your child has then developed the skills needed at this lower level, they can then move up with confidence. It is often better to begin at a lower level to build confidence as your child learns and develops their 11+ skills.

Non-verbal reasoning questions are different picture, pattern and shape puzzles. There are several different types of puzzles and the first part of this book looks at the different types and explains how to solve the puzzle.

When tackling non-verbal reasoning questions it is good to think about shapes and their position, and angle of any part, also the number, shading and size of parts within the pattern. **SPANSS** can help you to remember this list:

Shape

Position

Angle

Number

Shading

Size

1 Shape

KEY SKILLS

A key difference to look for in odd one out questions is shape. Look carefully at the patterns and images to see if there are any differences between their shapes.
Have any extra parts been added?
Is there one with a different shape to the others?

WORKED EXAMPLE

Which is the odd one out? Circle the letter.

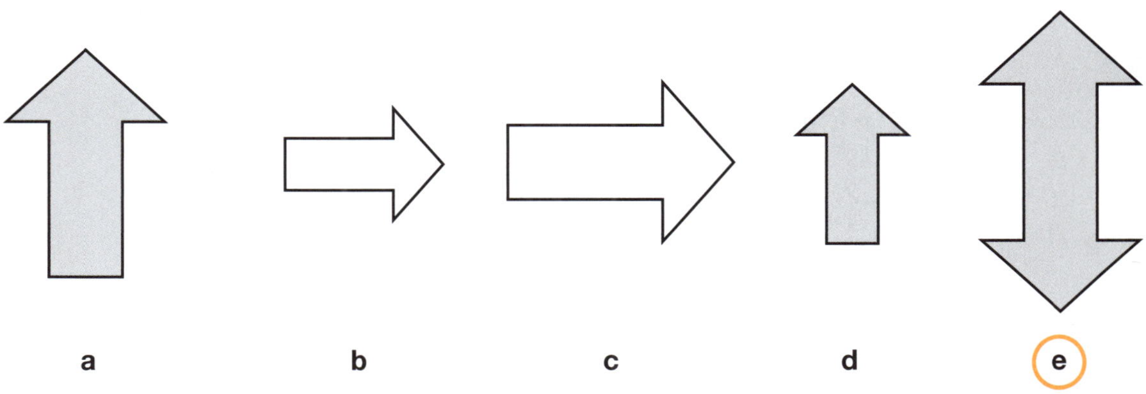

Three of the arrows are white and two are grey so that does not give an odd one out.
The arrows have been rotated in different ways but not giving one as the odd one out.
Looking at the shape, only one has an arrowhead at both ends.
So **option e** is the odd one out.

Now try these.

Which shape is the odd one out? Circle the letter.

1

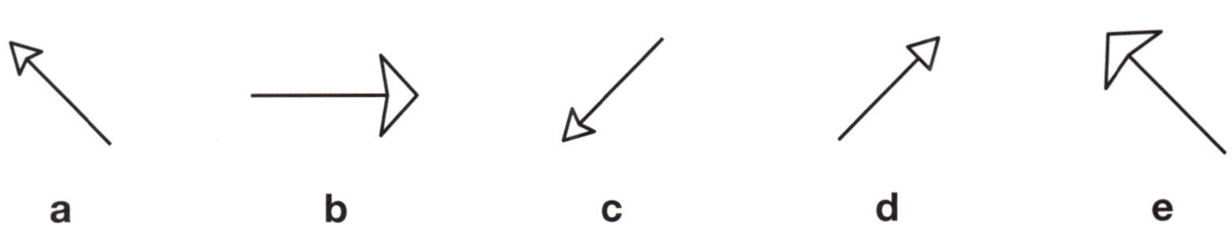

1

2

a b c d e

1

3

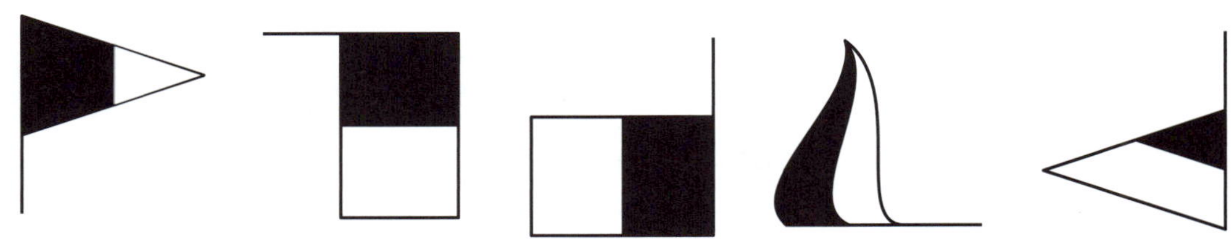

a b c d e

1

4

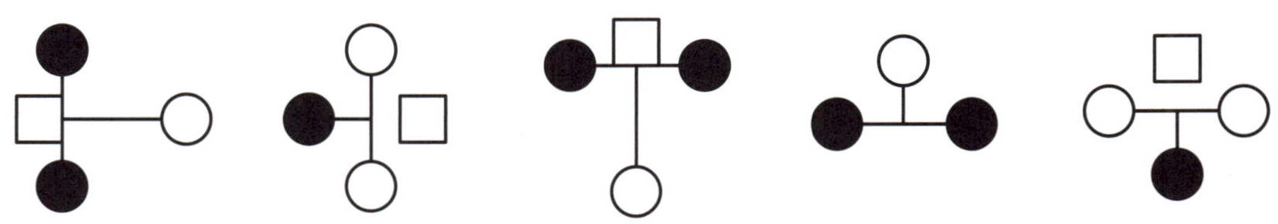

a b c d e

1

5

a b c d e

1

6

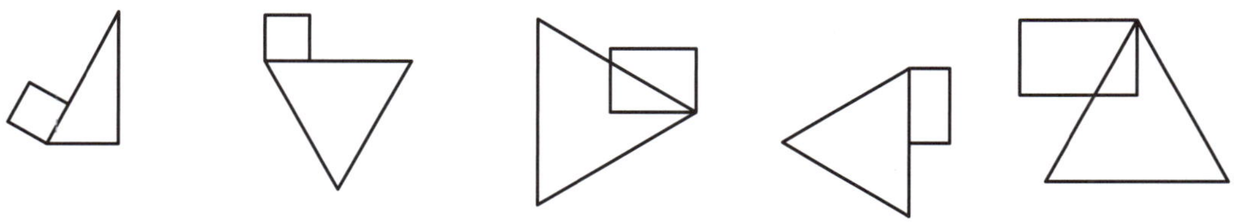

a b c d e

1

7

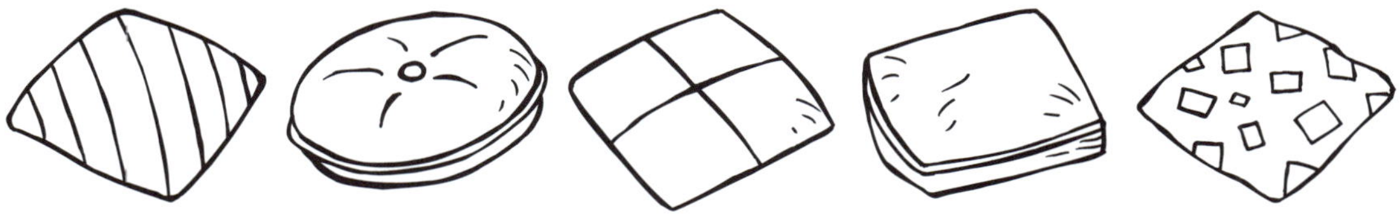

a b c d e

1

8

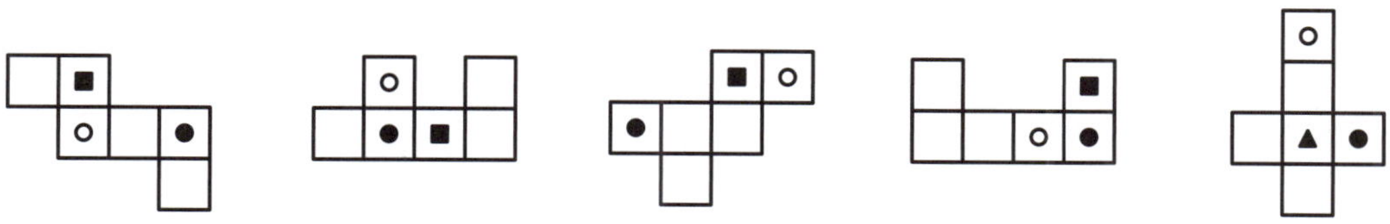

a b c d e

1

9

a b c d e

1

10

a b c d e

1

11

a b c d e

1

12

a b c d e

1

Total 12

2 Position

KEY SKILLS

Look carefully to see where key parts of a shape or image are located.
Are any parts of the image inside or outside other parts?
Are they above or below?
Are they in the centre or at the side?

WORKED EXAMPLE

Which is the odd one out? Circle the letter.

a **b** **c** **d** **e**

Three of the options have a pair of gloves and two have a hat, so that does not give an odd one out.
Four of the options have something on top of the table, and only one table has something underneath it. That gives **option d** as the odd one out.

Now try these.

Which is the odd one out? Circle the letter.

1

a **b** **c** **d** **e** 1

2

a **b** **c** **d** **e** 1

3

a b c d e

1

4

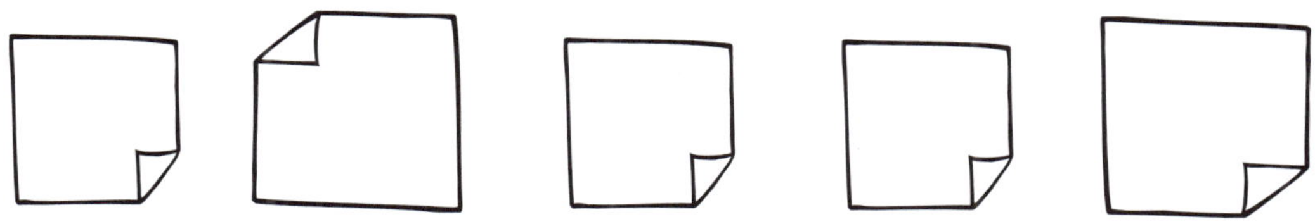

a b c d e

1

5

a b c d e

1

6

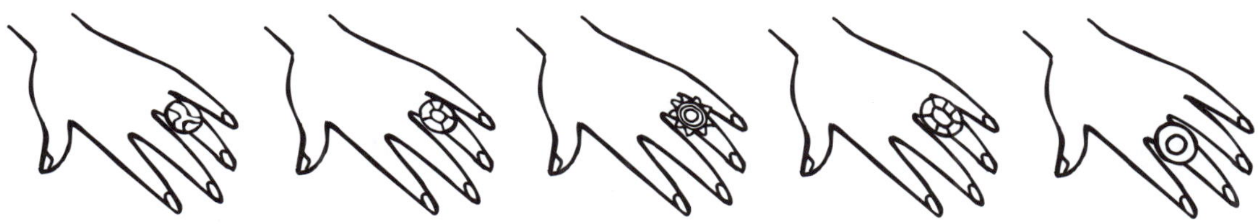

a b c d e

1

7

a b c d e

1

8

a b c d e

1

9

a b c d e

1

10

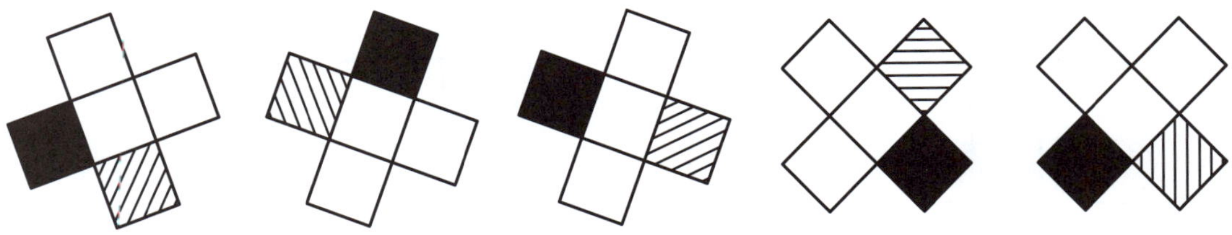

a b c d e

1

11

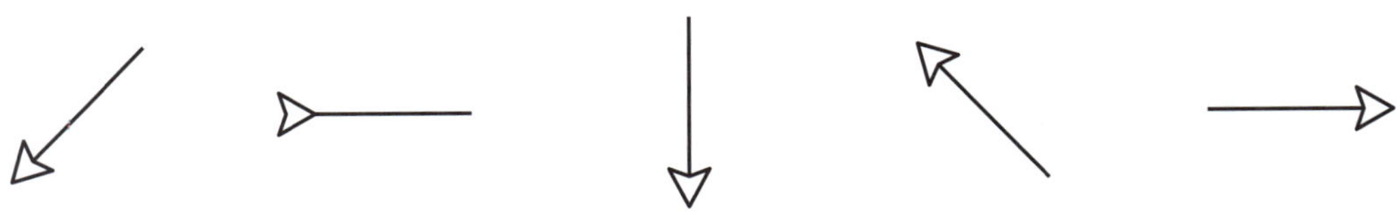

a b c d e

1

12

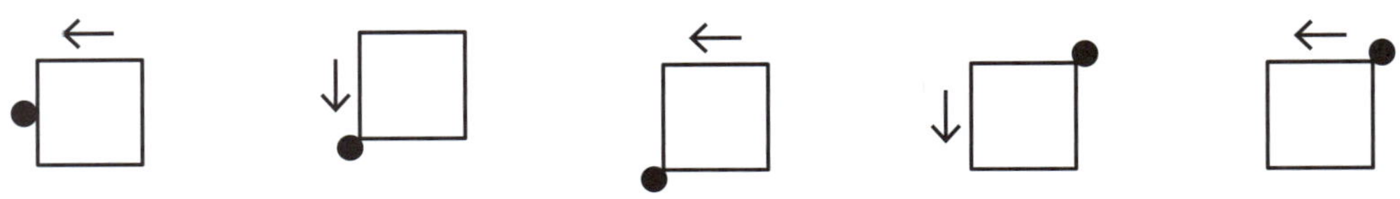

a b c d e

1

Total
12

3 Angle or Rotation

KEY SKILLS

Parts of an image or shape often form an angle, either on the page or in relation to another part of the image.
Are any of them **right angles**?
Have any of the shapes or parts of the shape been rotated?
Is the rotation clockwise or anti-clockwise?

WORKED EXAMPLE

Which is the odd one out? Circle the letter.

a b c d e

In this question all of the people are standing up straight and **vertical**.
They all have a shadow to the side.
Options a, b, c and d have the shadow forming an acute angle to the left.
Option e has the shadow forming a right angle to the right.
So **option e** is the odd one out.

Now try these.

Which is the odd one out? Circle the letter.

1

a b c d e

1

2

a b c d e

1

3

a b c d e

1

4

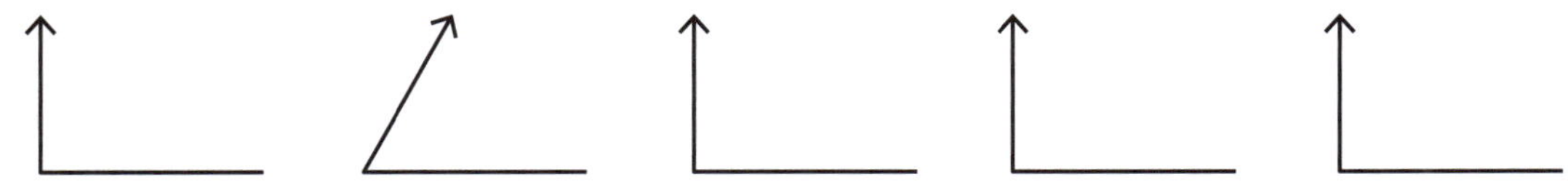

a b c d e

1

5

a b c d e

1

6

a b c d e

1

7

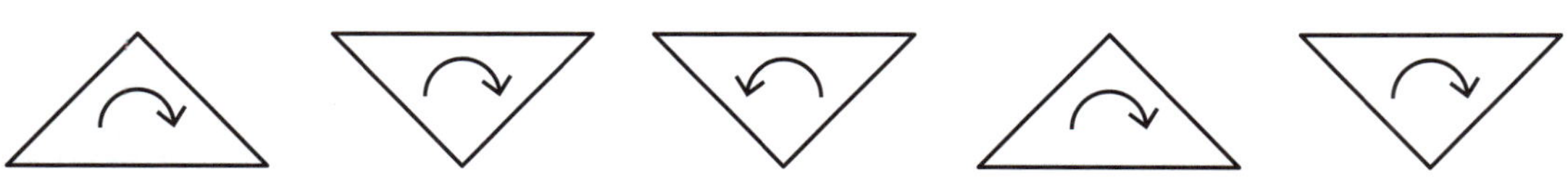

a b c d e

1

8

a b c d e

1

9

a b c d e

1

10

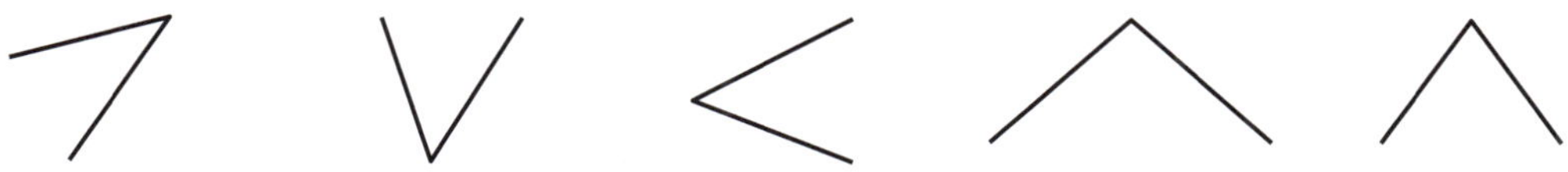

a b c d e

1

11

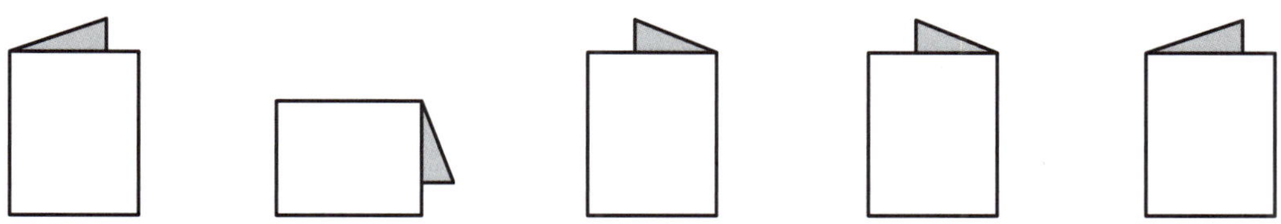

a b c d e

1

12

a b c d e

1

Total
12

4 Number

KEY SKILLS

Look carefully at pictures and patterns in a question.
Are there repeated lines or shapes to count?
Are there objects where patterns have different numbers of parts?

WORKED EXAMPLES

Which is the odd one out? Circle the letter.

a b (c) d e

How many eggs are there in each box?
There are 6 in each box.
How many of the eggs are white?
Options a, b, d and e all have four white eggs, option c has six.
So **option c** is the odd one out.

Now try these.

Which is the odd one out? Circle the letter.

1

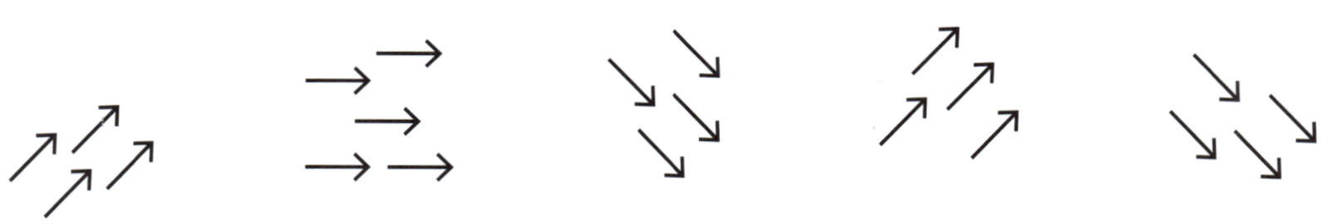

a b c d e 1

2

a b c d e 1

3

a b c d e

1

4

a b c d e

1

5

a b c d e

1

6

a b c d e

1

7

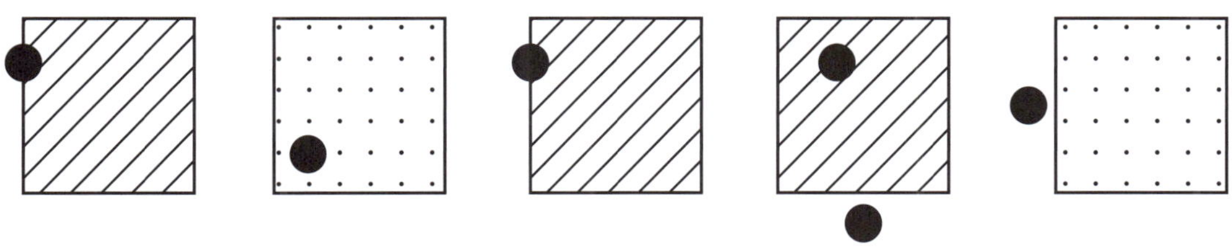

a b c d e

1

8

a b c d e

1

9

a b c d e

1

10

a b c d e

1

11

a b c d e

1

12

a b c d e

1

Total 12

5 Shading

KEY SKILLS

Shapes and patterns often have parts shaded in. If it is line shading, look carefully at the direction of the lines.
Is there any shading?
Do all the shapes have the same type of shading?
If they are different, is there an odd one out?

WORKED EXAMPLE

Which is the odd one out? Circle the letter.

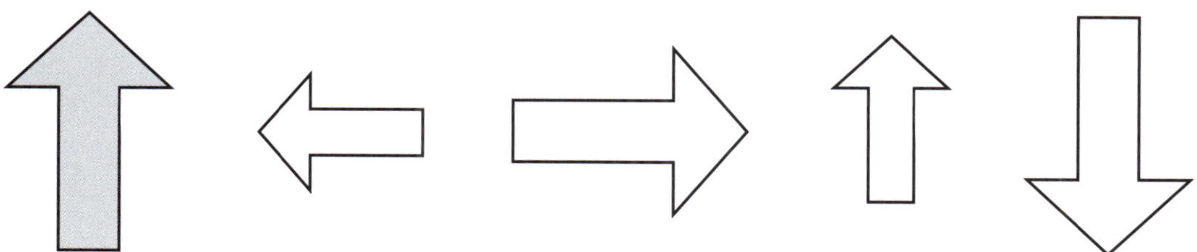

(a) b c d e

Angle The arrows are rotated in different ways but there is not an odd one out.
Size There are three large and two small arrows so there is not an odd one out.
Shading Only option a is shaded grey, the others are white.
So **option a** is the odd one out.

Now try these.

Which is the odd one out? Circle the letter.

1

a b c d e

1

2

a b c d e

1

3

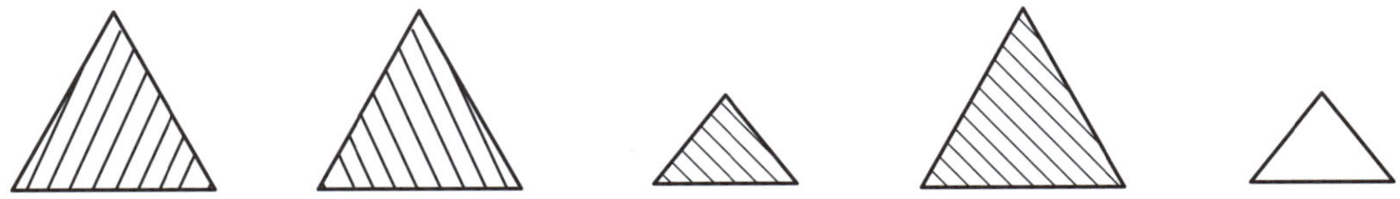

a b c d e 1

4

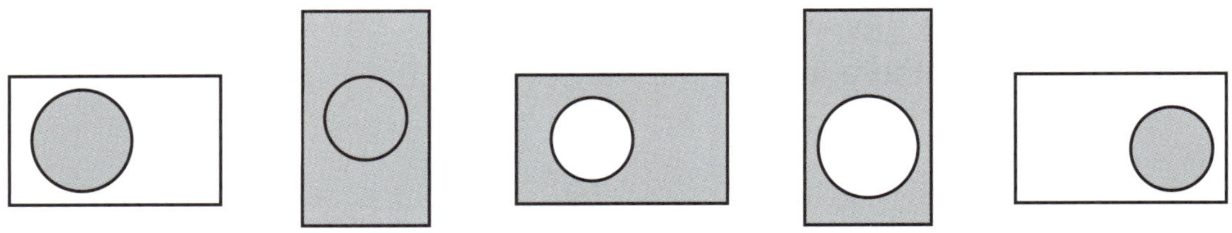

a b c d e 1

5

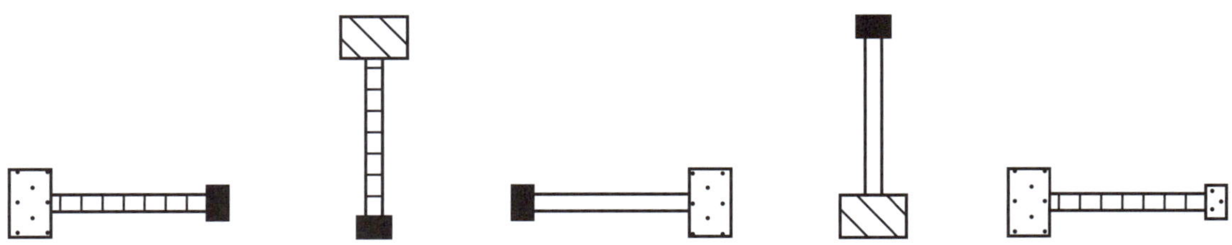

a b c d e 1

6

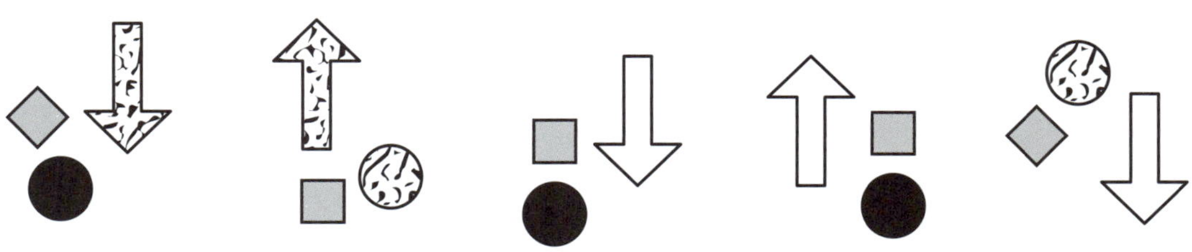

a b c d e 1

7

a b c d e 1

8

a b c d e 1

9

a b c d e

1

10

a b c d e

1

11

a b c d e

1

12

a b c d e

1

Total 12

6 Size

KEY SKILLS

A key difference to look for in odd one out questions is size.
Are all of the shapes the same size?
Are all of the parts the same size in each pattern?

WORKED EXAMPLE

Which is the odd one out? Circle the letter.

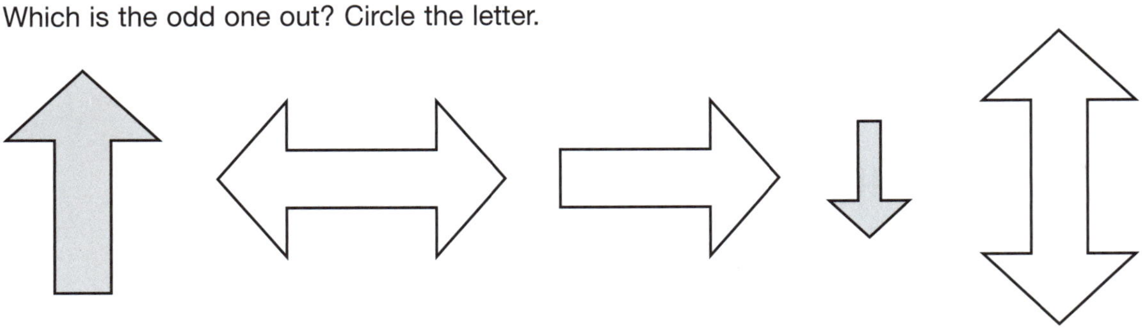

a b c d e

Angle The arrows are rotated in different ways but there is not an odd one out.
Shading Two are grey and one is white, so there is not an odd one out.
Size Four are large and only one is small.
So **option d**, the small arrow, is the odd one out.

Now try these.

Which is the odd one out? Circle the letter.

1

a b c d e

1

2

a b c d e

1

3

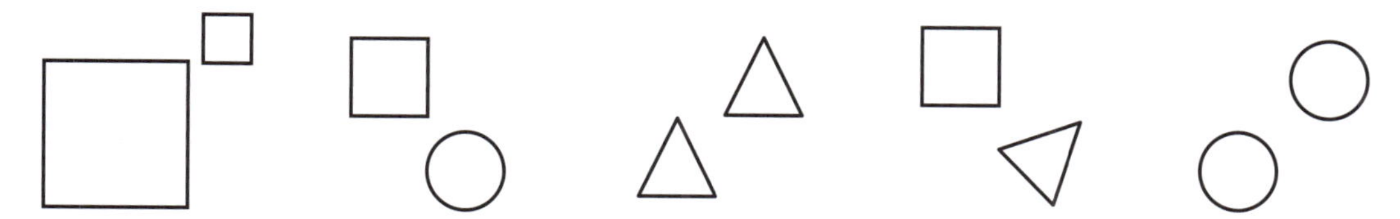

a b c d e

1 ☐

4

a b c d e

1 ☐

5

a b c d e

1 ☐

6

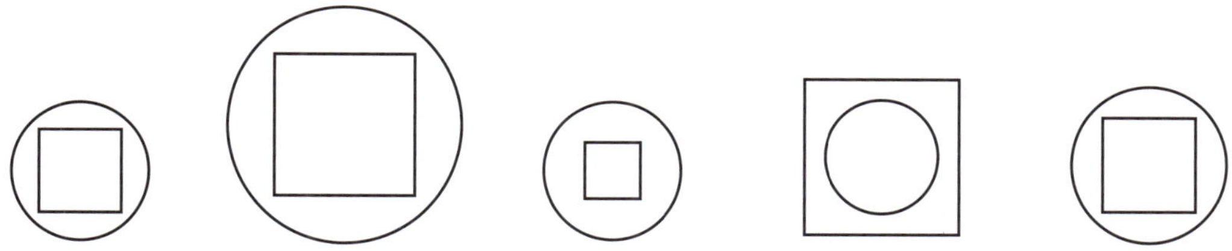

a b c d e

1 ☐

7

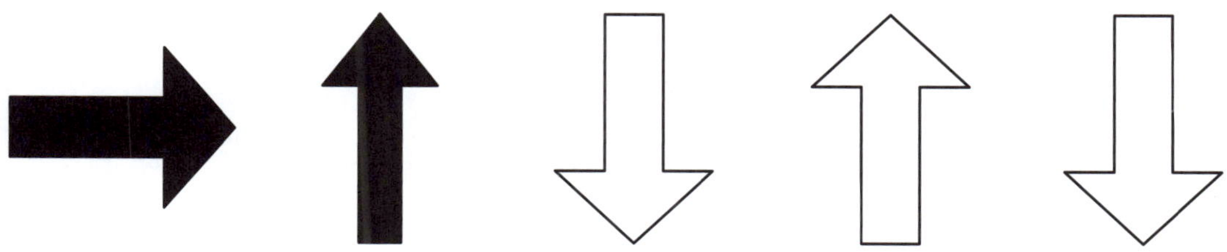

a b c d e

1 ☐

8

a b c d e

1 ☐

9

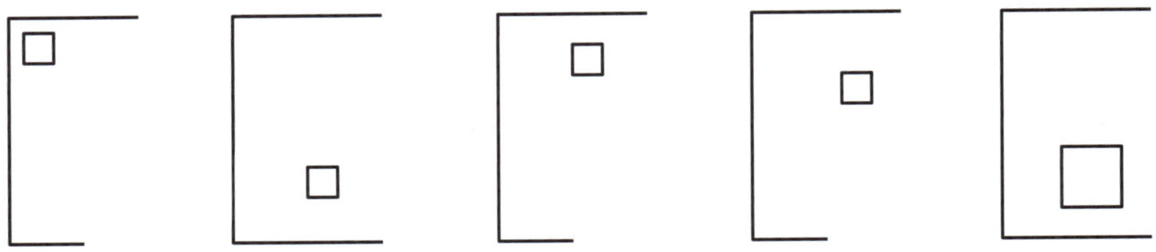

a b c d e

1

10

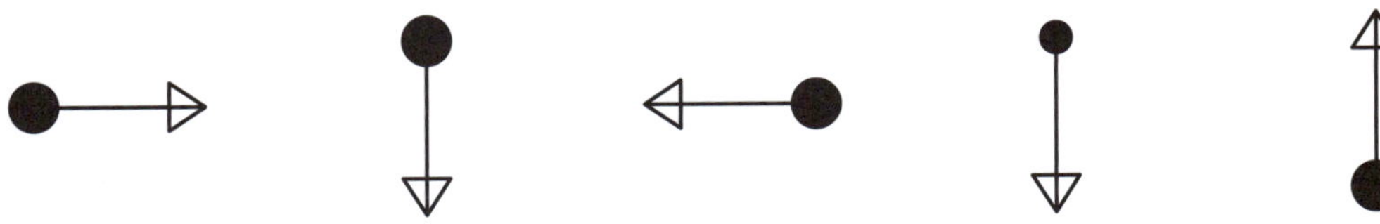

a b c d e

1

11

a b c d e

1

12

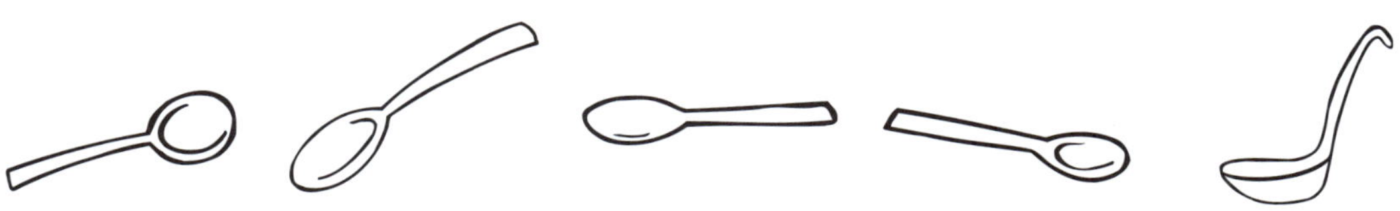

a b c d e

1

Total
12

7 Similarities

KEY SKILLS

In these questions you are given a group of shapes or patterns. You have to look at them carefully to work out how they are all similar. Then see which of the answer options given is similar in the same way.

TOP TIP!

Remember the acronym **SPANSS** to help answer these types of questions.

1 **S**hape **2** **P**osition **3** **A**ngle **4** **N**umber **5** **S**hading **6** **S**ize

Make up your own prompt (mnemonic) to help you remember.
For example, Spotty Pyjamas And Nice Soft Slippers.

WORKED EXAMPLE

Which one on the right belongs to the group on the left? Circle the letter.

a b c d e

How are the shapes on the left all similar?
They are all faces.
All have two open eyes, no nose and smiles.
Some have hats and some have hair.

To belong, the shapes have to be a face with two open eyes and a smile.
a has a nose and no smile.
b has two eyes closed.
c has two open eyes, a smile and no nose, so could be the answer.

Check the other options:
d has one open eye and no smile.
e has two open eyes but no smile.
So **option c** is the answer.

Now try these.

Which one on the right belongs to the group on the left? Circle the letter.

1

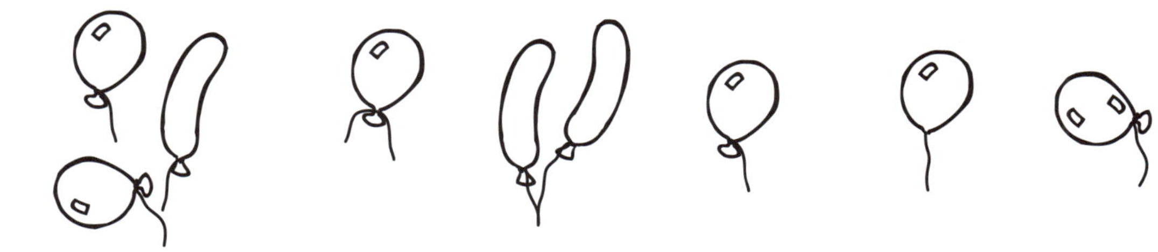

a b c d e

1

2

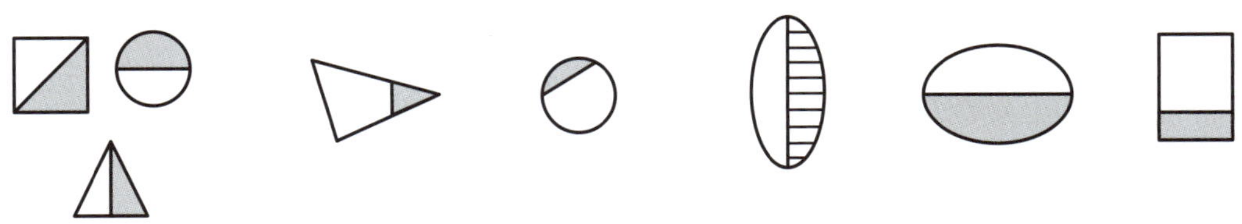

a b c d e

1

3

a b c d e

1

4

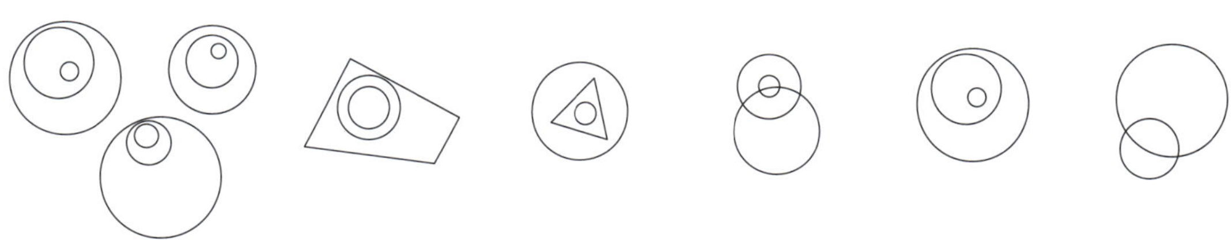

a b c d e

1

5

a b c d e

1

6

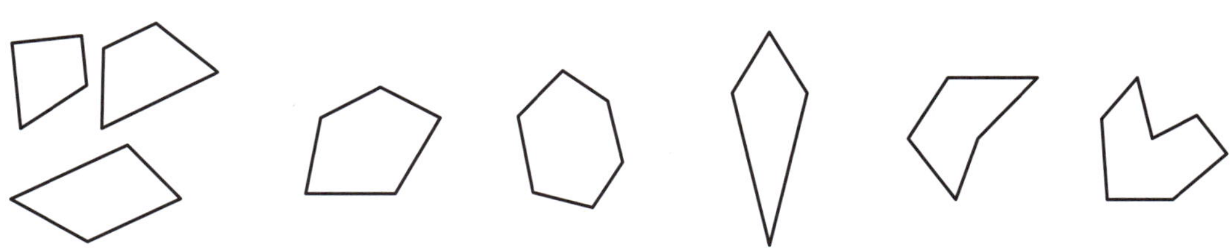

a b c d e

1

7

a b c d e

1

8

a b c d e

1

9

a b c d e

1

10

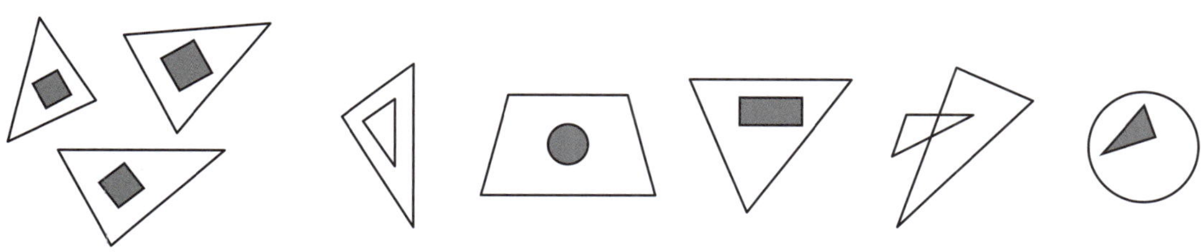

a b c d e

1

11

a b c d e

1

12

a b c d e

1

Total
12

8 Analogies or Pairing Up

KEY SKILLS

In this type of question, you are given a pair of shapes or pictures. Look carefully to see the connection between them or work out how the first shape has been changed to give the second shape. After working out the link, complete the second pair of pictures or shapes using the same link. With picture questions of this type look for the connection or link between them. When the question has shapes using SPANSS (Shape, Position, Angle, Number, Shading, Size) can help you to spot how the first shape has been changed to give the second shape.

WORKED EXAMPLE

Which one completes the second pair in the same way as the first pair?
Circle the letter.

 is to  as  is to **?**

a (circled)

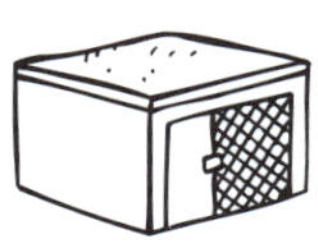

b

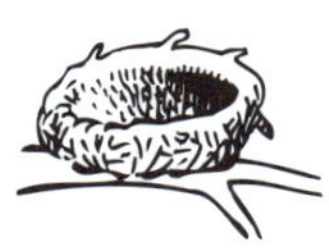

c

d

e

The first pair shows a dog with a kennel, which is a place where dogs sometimes live. So the link is that what is shown in the first picture can live in what is shown in the second picture.

A fish lives in water – could be the sea, a lake or pond, a river or a fish tank. Looking at the answer options only option a has water, so **option a** is the answer.

TOP TIP!

It is a good idea to check all of the answer options to make sure it is the correct answer.

Now try these.

Which one completes the second pair in the same way as the first pair? Circle the letter.

1  is to  as  is to **?**

a b c d e

1

2  is to  as  is to **?**

a b c d e

1

3  is to  as  is to **?**

a b c d e

1

4  is to  as  is to **?**

a b c d e

1

5  is to  as  is to **?**

 **a**  **b**  **c**  **d**  **e**

1

6  is to  as  is to **?**

 **a**  **b**  **c**  **d**  **e**

1

7  is to  as  is to **?**

 **a**  **b**  **c**  **d**  **e**

1

8  is to  as  is to **?**

 **a**  **b**  **c**  **d**  **e**

1

9  is to  as  is to **?**

a **b** **c** **d** **e**

1

10  is to  as  is to **?**

a **b** **c** **d** **e**

1

11  is to  as  is to **?**

a **b** **c** **d** **e**

1

12 

is to 

as 

is to **?**

a **b** **c** **d** **e**

1

Total 12

9 Reflections

KEY SKILLS

In these questions, find the picture or shape that is a reflection of the first shape or picture. Use a mirror to find the reflections. The dotted line, which is the line of reflection, is the mirror line.

A correct pair is shown below.

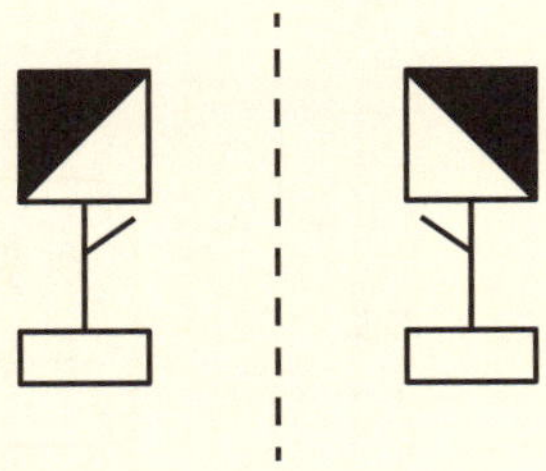

All the key points on the object on the left should be the same distance away from the mirror line.

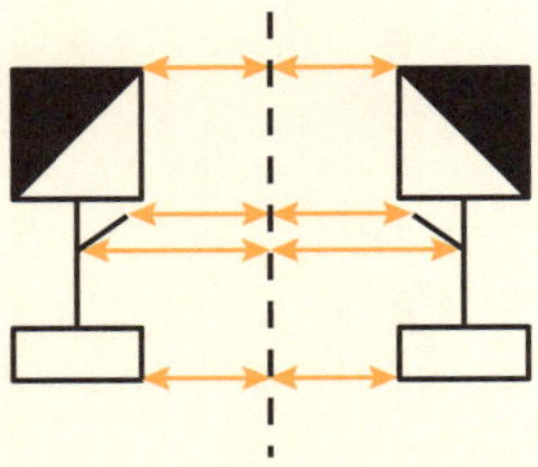

TOP TIP!

Some people prefer to look at these rotated. Some people do not mind which way around it is. If you prefer the right hand version, you should rotate the book around for these questions.

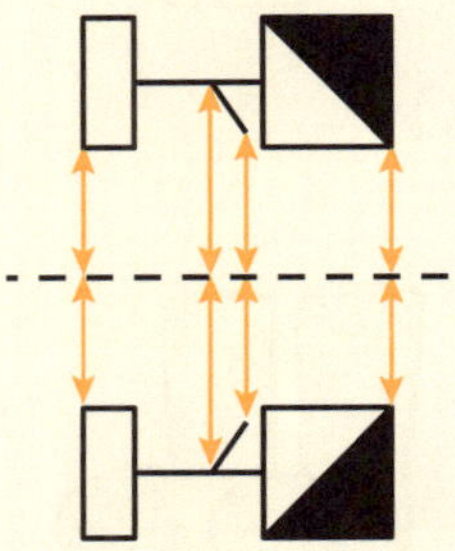

WORKED EXAMPLE

Which shape on the right is the reflection of the shape given on the left? Circle the letter.

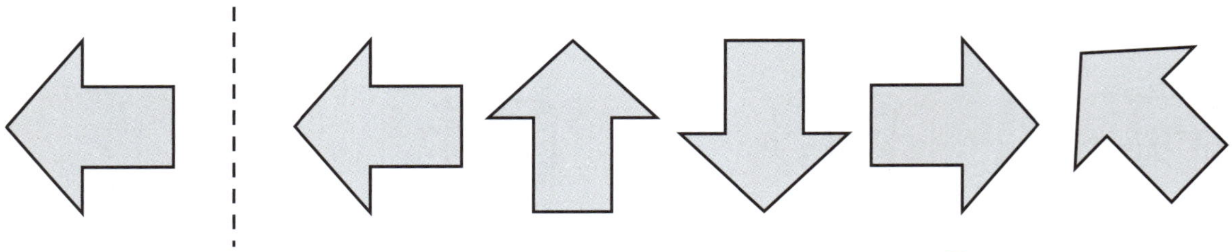

a b c (d) e

The arrow points to the left away from the mirror line. This means that the correct answer will also point away in the opposite direction.

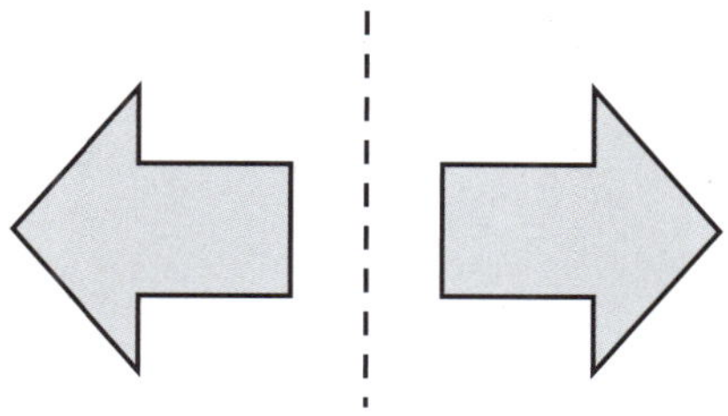

Now try these.

Which one on the right is a reflection of the one on the left? Circle the letter.

1

a b c d e

1

2

a b c d e

1

3

a b c d e

1

4

a b c d e

1

5

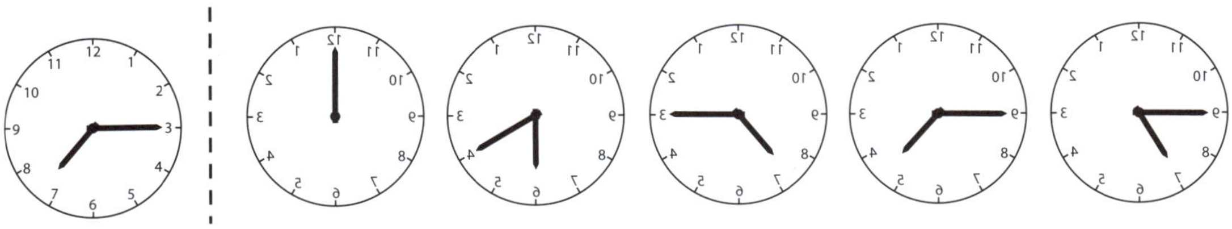

a b c d e

1

6

a b c d e

1

7

a b c d e

1

8

a b c d e

1

9

a b c d e

1

10

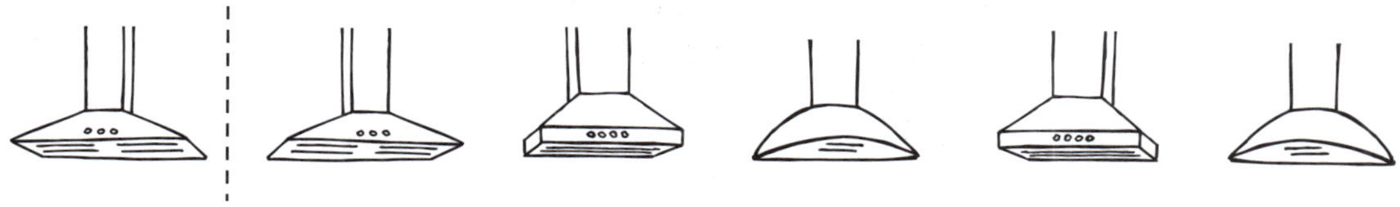

a b c d e

1

11

a b c d e

1

12

a b c d e

1

Total 12

10 Grids

KEY SKILLS

In these questions, find the picture or shape that completes the square grid. There may be a repeating pattern or sequence that goes along the rows or down the columns. Or the whole grid may make up a pattern, with one half being a reflection of the other half or shapes being rotated around the grid. Check each answer option carefully.

WORKED EXAMPLE

Which shape or pattern completes the larger square? Circle the letter.

1

a b (c) d e

Here there is a pattern alternating between an apple and a pear, both along the rows and down the columns. So the correct answer is **option c**.

Now try these.

Which shape or pattern completes the larger square? Circle the letter.

1

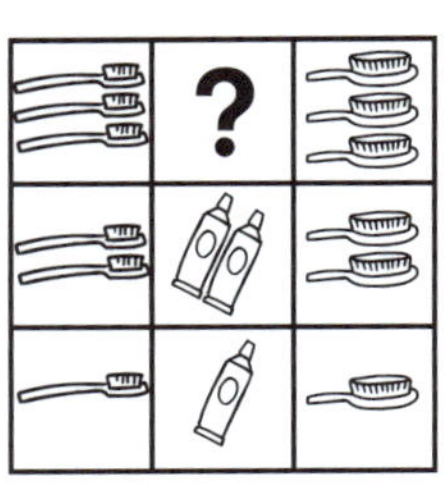

a b c d e

1

2

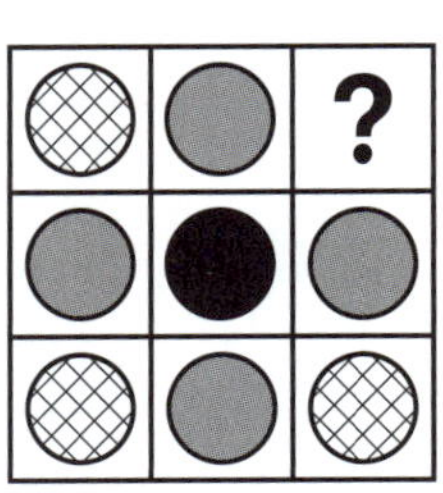

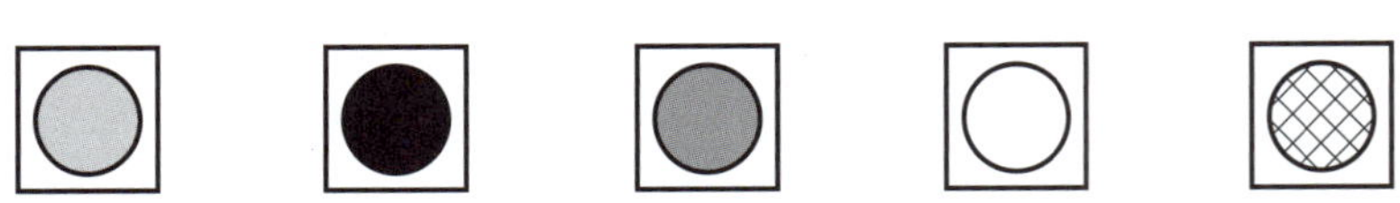

a b c d e

1

3

a b c d e

1

4

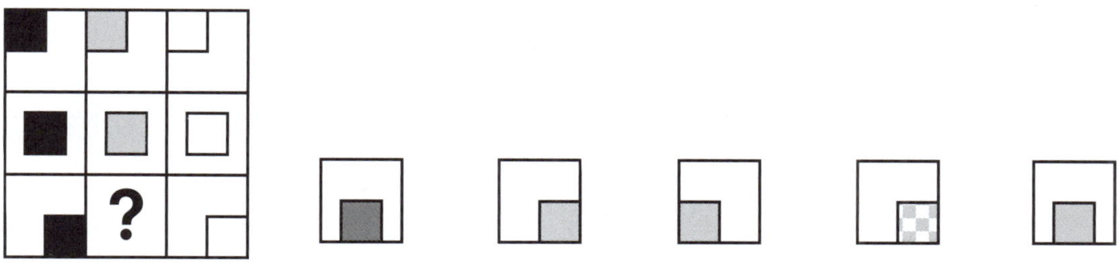

a b c d e

1

5

a b c d e

1

6

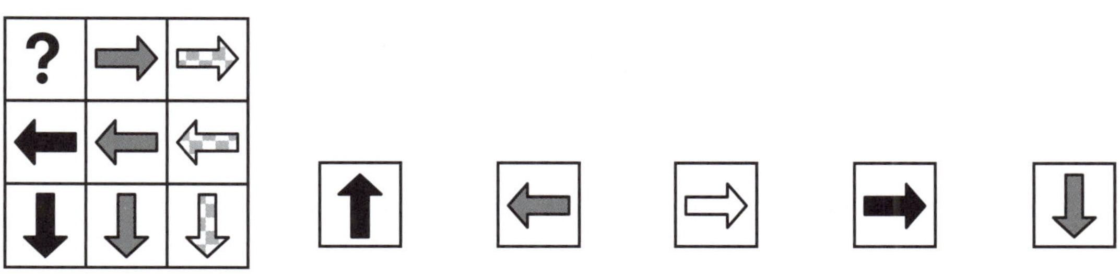

a b c d e

1

7

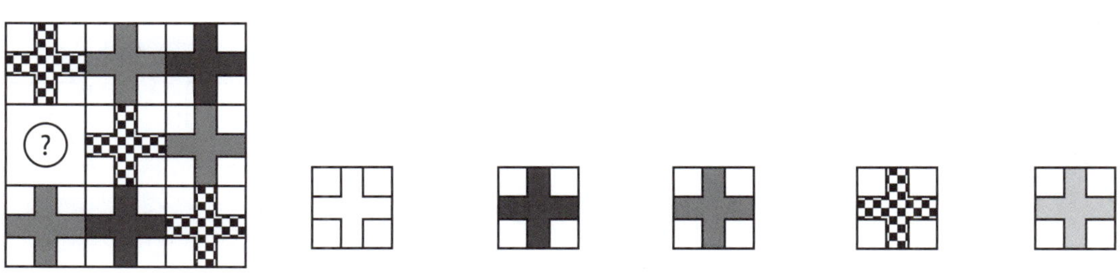

a b c d e

1

8

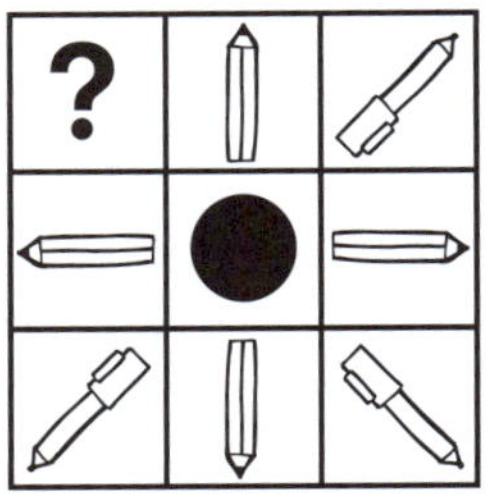

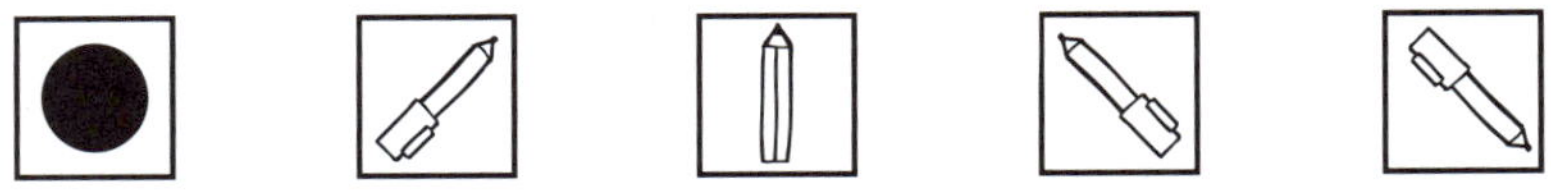

a b c d e

1

9

a b c d e

1

10

a b c d e

1

11

a b c d e

1

12

a b c d e

1

Total 12

11 Sequences

KEY SKILLS

These questions ask which shapes or pictures come next.
Some sequences are made up of repeated patterns. Have a look at the first picture and see if it is repeated anywhere else. Then check the second shape – is it also repeated after the first one? Check each shape to find the block of repeating shapes.

This is a two repeat:

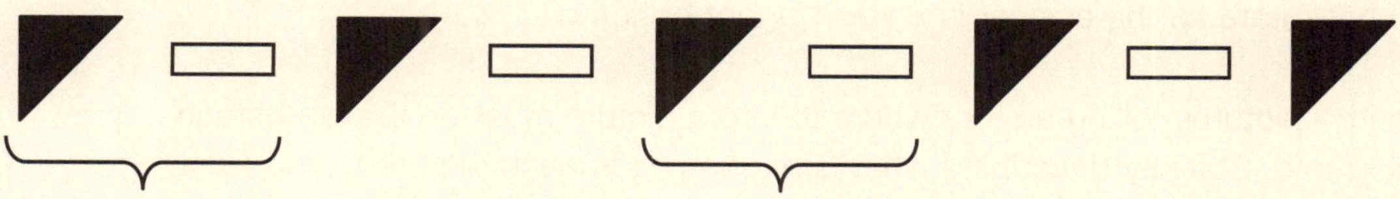

This is a three repeat:

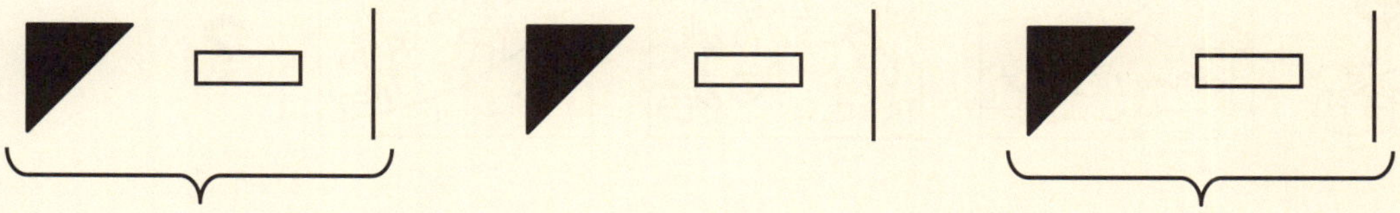

WORKED EXAMPLES

Which shape or pattern completes the sequence? Circle the letter.

1

a b c d e

Check each shape carefully – do not get caught out if one shape is repeated within the repeating block of shapes.

Or there may be elements of the sequence which repeat with different frequencies:

2  ?

(a) b c d e

Here triangles **alternate** with rectangles, and the shading style follows a repeating pattern of three – checked-white-black. So the next shape will be a black triangle. The shapes do not rotate so the answer is **option a**, not option d.

A sequence can be pictures telling a story where the next picture must be the next stage in the story being told. Start by describing what is happening in each picture.

3  ?

a b c d e

What is happening?

Packing a bag Driving off in the car Putting on boots Climbing up a hill

Now look at the answer options and describe them:

a walking down the hill

b at the top of the hill

c leaving the car

d returning to the car

e driving home

As the last picture given shows them climbing the hill, they have already left the car so the answer cannot be option c. Then before walking down and returning to the car they still get to the top of the hill, so the next picture is **option b**.

Now try these.

Which one comes next? Circle the letter.

1

 **?**

a b c d e

1

2

 **?**

a b c d e

1

3

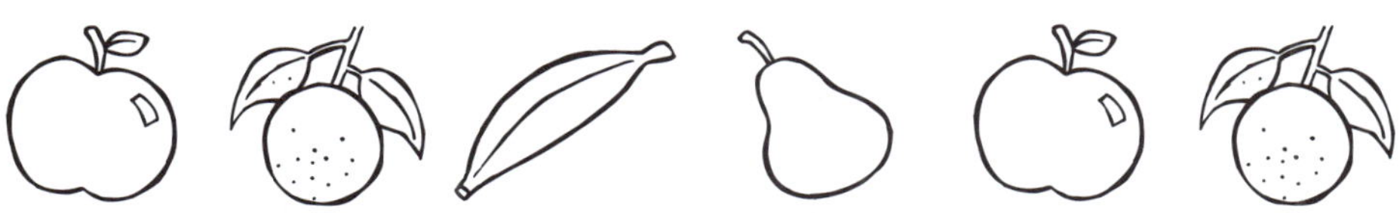 **?**

a b c d e

1

4

 **?**

a b c d e

1

5

a b c d e

1

6

a b c d e

1

7

a b c d e

1

8

a b c d e

1

9

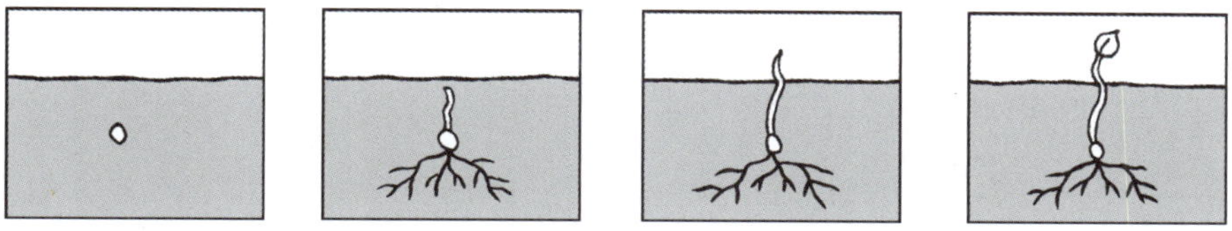

?

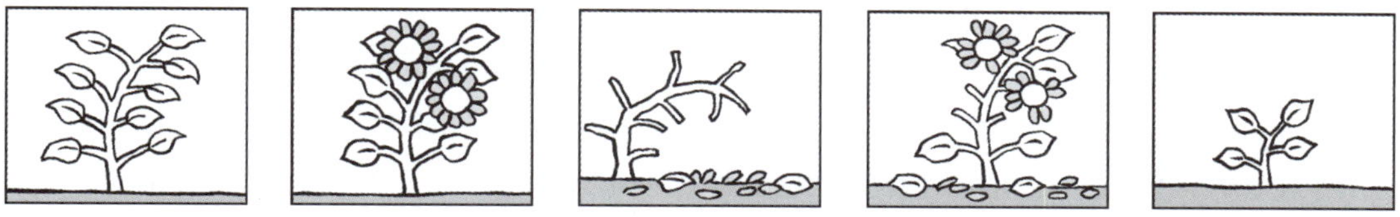

a b c d e

1

10

?

a b c d e

1

11

?

a b c d e

1

12

?

a b c d e

1

Total 12

12 Hidden shapes and Combining shapes

KEY SKILLS

In these questions look carefully at shapes. In the hidden shape questions find the picture or pattern where that exact shape is included. When combining two shapes the two separate shapes on the left must not change when they are put together. The shading and number of lines must stay the same, but they may be rotated. Combining shapes is explained in more detail on the next page.

Hidden shapes:

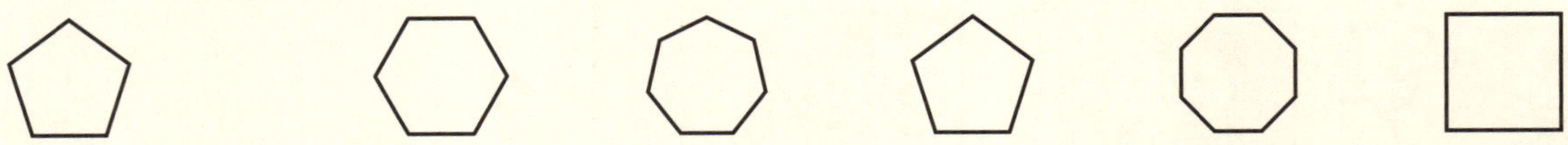

a b (c) d e

Here we can see that c is the same as the object on the left.

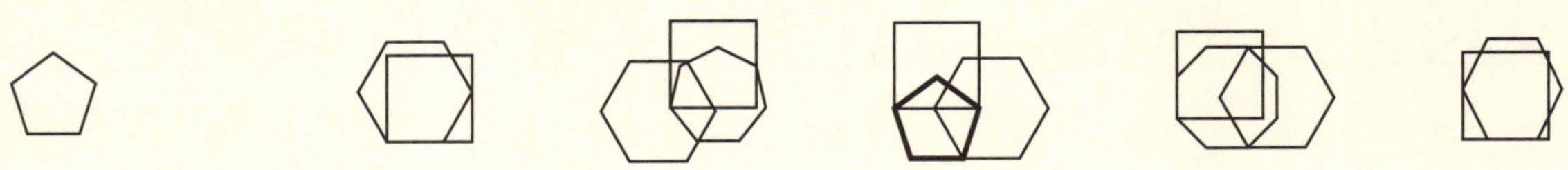

a b (c) d e

Combining shapes:
In these questions there are two shapes on the left and these are put together to make one of the shapes on the right. The shapes do not change in size or shading but might be rotated. Start by looking for the first shape in each of the options. It can help to go over the shape in pencil and cross out any of the options which do not contain it. Now in the shapes left can you see the second shape?
Remember there will not be any extra lines but the shape may be rotated. Drawing over the shape in pencil is a good way to check it.

WORKED EXAMPLES

1 In which larger shape is the shape on the left hidden? Circle the letter.

a b c (d) e

All the wheels on the other pictures do not have the two inner rings and do not have the extra bits on the outside.

2 Which shape on the right is made up of the two shapes on the left? Circle the letter.

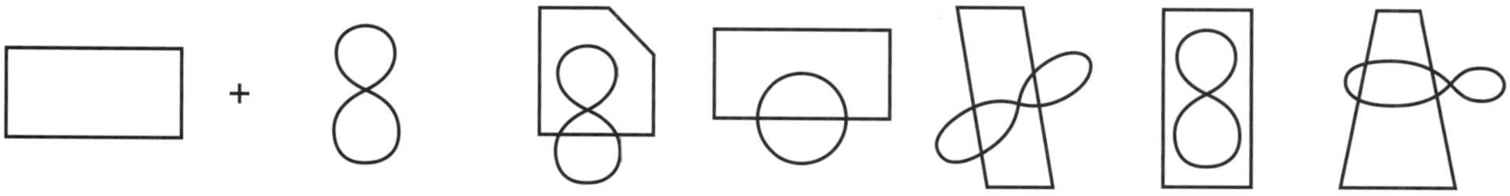

a b c d e

Here are two shapes. The first shape is found in options b and d, so options a, c and e can be crossed out.
Then look at the second shape, is it in option b or option d? It only appears in option d, so **option d** is the answer.

Now try these.

In which shape or picture on the right is the shape or picture on the left hidden? Circle the letter.

1

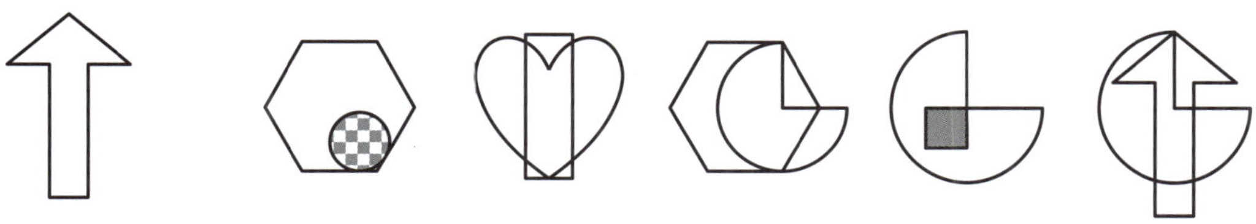

a b c d e 1

2

a b c d e 1

3

a b c d e 1

4

a b c d e 1

5

a b c d e

1

6

a b c d e

1

Which shape on the right is made up of the two shapes on the left?
Circle the letter.

7

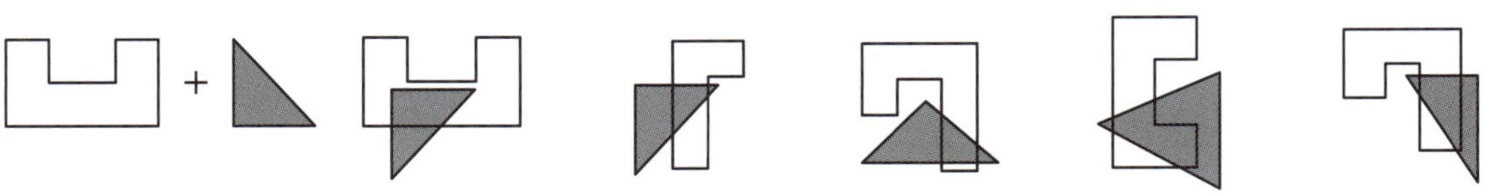

a b c d e

1

8

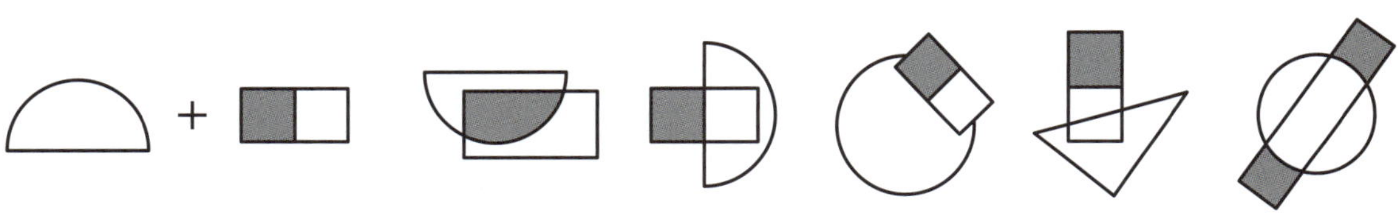

a b c d e

1

9

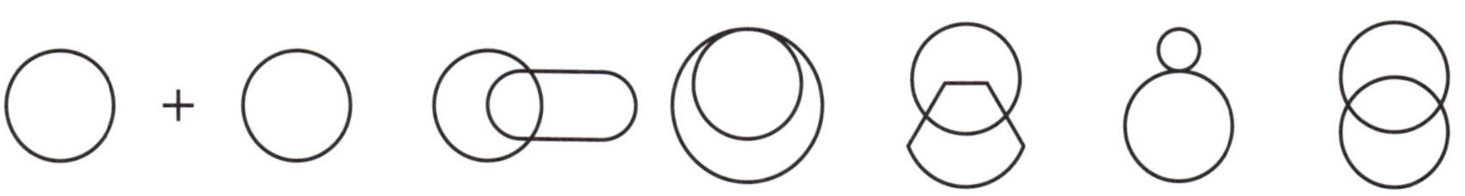

a b c d e

1

10

a b c d e

1

11

a b c d e

1

12

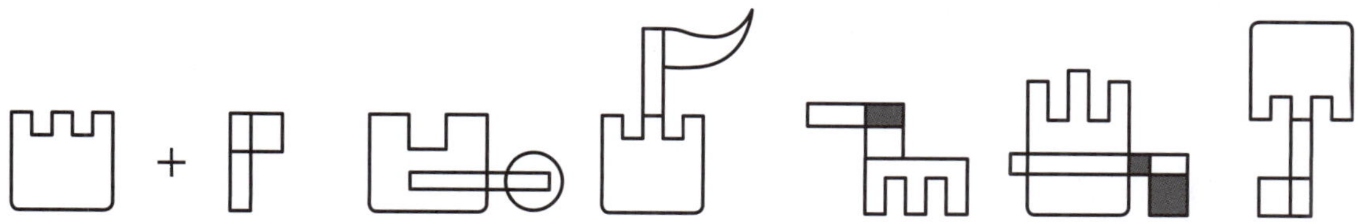

a b c d e

1

Total 12

Puzzle 1

Puzzle 1

Which one comes next? Circle the letter.

1

a b c d e

1

2

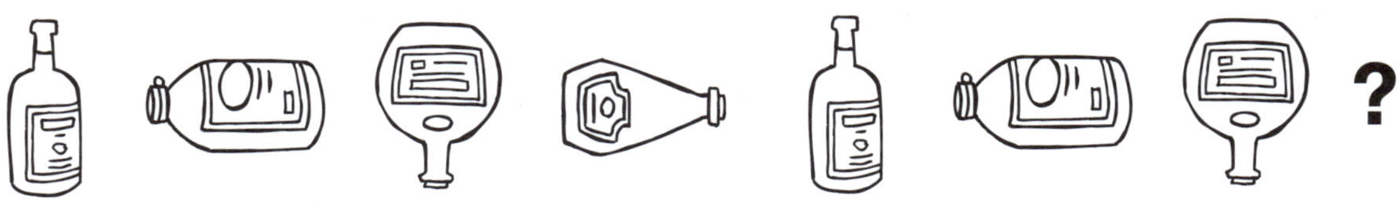

a b c d e

1

Which picture on the right is the reflection of the picture given on the left, in the dotted mirror line? Circle the letter.

3

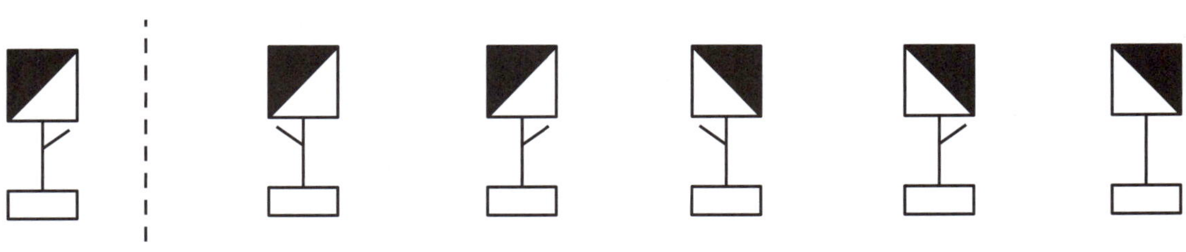

a b c d e

1

4

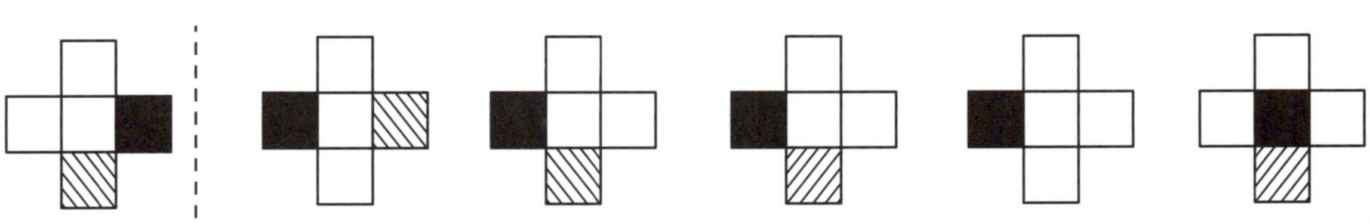

a b c d e

1

Total 4

Mixed Paper 1

Which is the odd one out? Circle the letter.

1

a b c d e

1

2

a b c d e

1

3

a b c d e

1

4

a b c d e

1

Which one on the right belongs to the group on the left? Circle the letter.

5

 a
 b
 c
 d
 e

1

6

 a
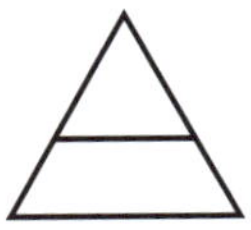 b
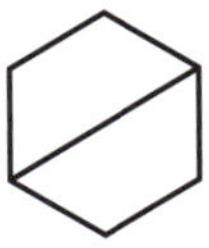 c
 d
 e

1

7
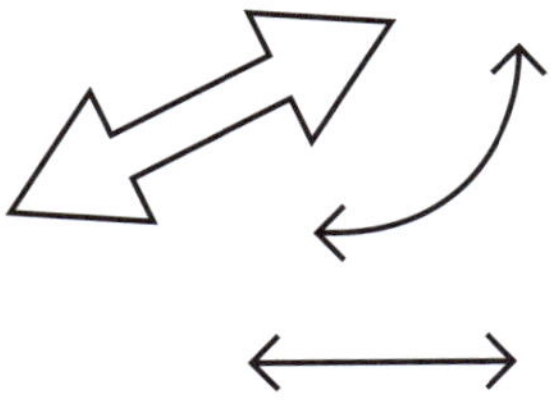

 a
 b
 c
 d
 e

1

Which one completes the second pair in the same way as the first pair? Circle the letter.

8  is to  as  is to **?**

 a
 b
 c
 d
 e

1

9  is to  as  is to **?**

 **a** 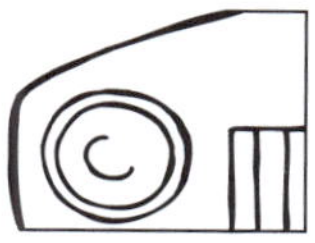 **b**  **c**  **d**  **e**

1

10  is to  as  is to **?**

 **a**  **b**  **c**  **d**  **e**

1

11 ab is to ba as cd is to **?**

a	b	c	d	e
cc	dd	cd	dc	ac

1

12  is to  as 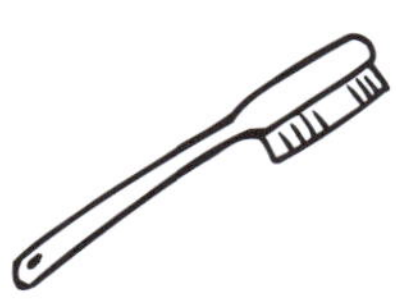 is to **?**

 **a** 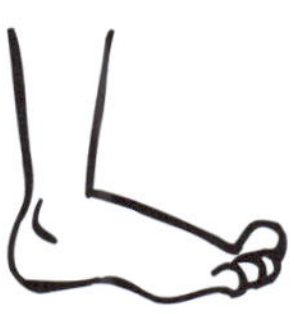 **b**  **c** 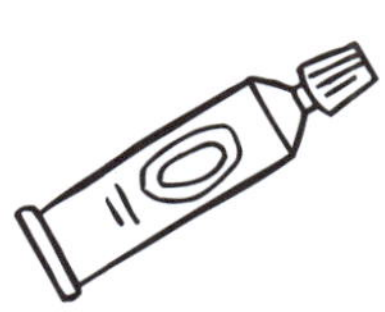 **d**  **e**

1

13  is to  as  is to **?**

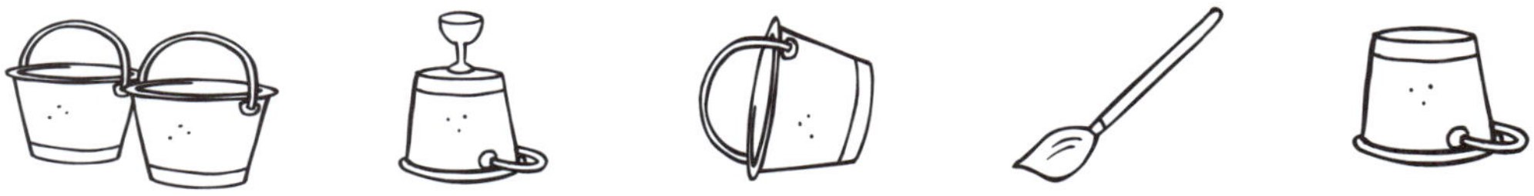

a **b** **c** **d** **e**

1

14 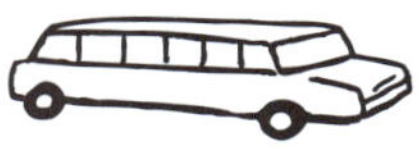 is to  as  is to **?**

a **b** **c** **d** **e**

1

Which picture on the right is a reflection of the picture on the left, in the dotted mirror line? Circle the letter.

15

a **b** **c** **d** **e**

1

16

a **b** **c** **d** **e**

1

17

a **b** **c** **d** **e**

1

Mixed Papers

Mixed Paper 1

Which one comes next? Circle the letter.

18

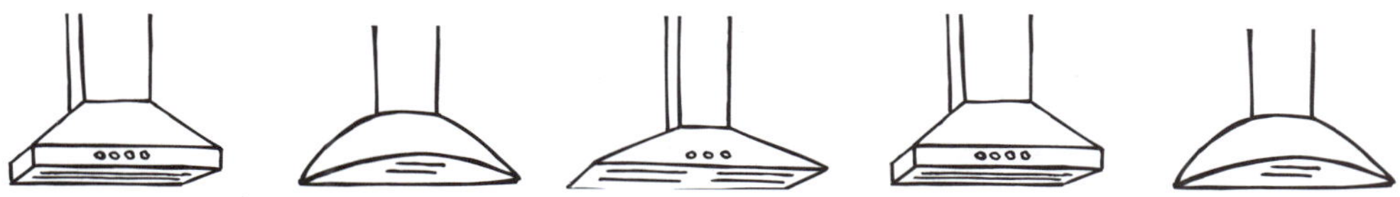

a b c d e

1

19

a b c d e

1

20

a b c d e

1

Total 20

Mixed Paper 2

In which larger picture is the smaller picture hidden? Circle the letter.

1

a b c d e

1

2

a b c d e

1

3

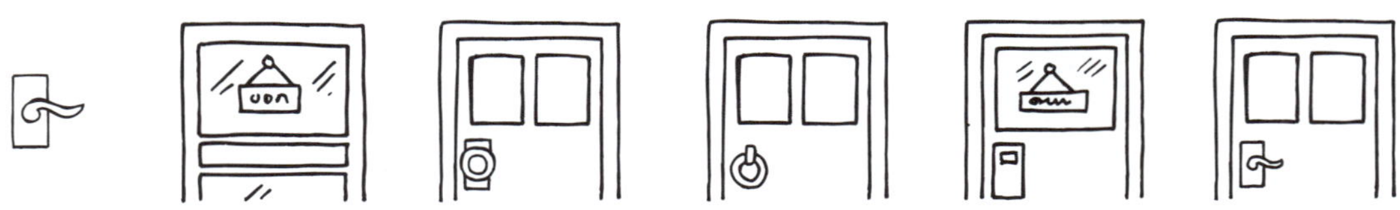

a b c d e

1

Which one comes next? Circle the letter.

4

a b c d e

1

5

a b c d e

1

6

a b c d e

1

Which is the odd one out? Circle the letter.

7

a b c d e

1

8

a b c d e

1

9

a b c d e

1

10

a b c d e

1

11

a b c d e

1

Which picture completes the second pair in the same way as the first pair?
Circle the letter.

12  is to  as  is to **?**

a **b** **c** **d** **e**

1

13  is to  as  is to **?**

a **b** **c** **d** **e**

1

14  is to  as  is to **?**

a **b** **c** **d** **e**

1

Which shape on the right is made up of the two shapes on the left?
Circle the letter.

15  + 

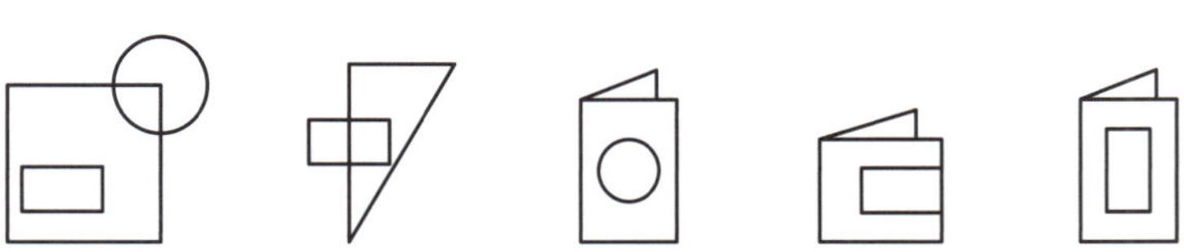

a **b** **c** **d** **e**

1

16

a b c d e

1

17

a b c d e

1

Which shape on the right completes the square grid on the left? Circle the letter.

18

a b c d e

1

19

a b c d e

1

20

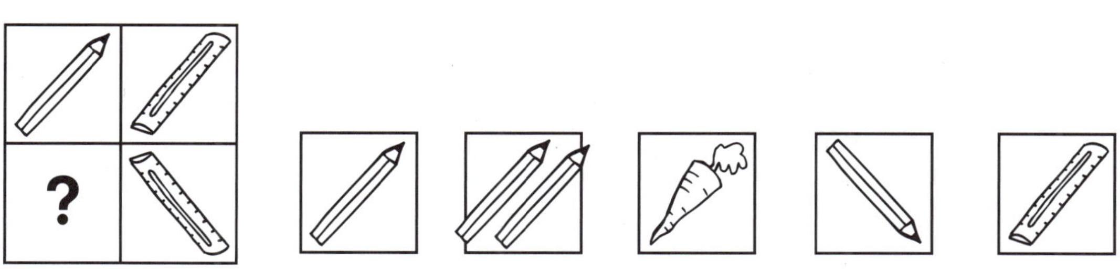

a b c d e

1

Total 20

Mixed Paper 3

Which one comes next? Circle the letter.

1

a b c d e

1

2

a b c d e

1

3

a b c d e

1

4

a b c d e

1

5

?

a b c d e

1

6

?

a b c d e

1

Which is the odd one out? Circle the letter.

7

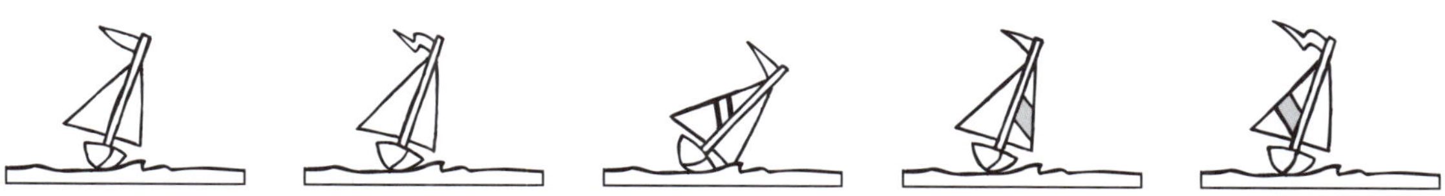

a b c d e

1

8

a b c d e

1

Which one completes the larger square on the left? Circle the letter.

9

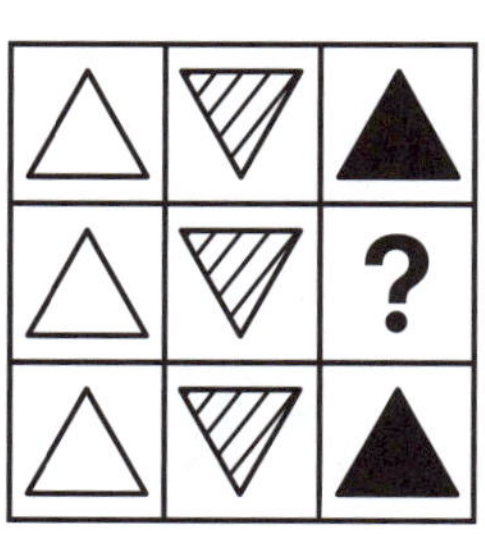

a b c d e

1

Mixed Paper 3

10 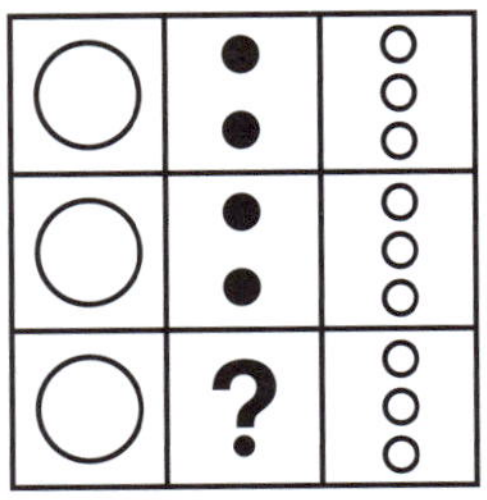

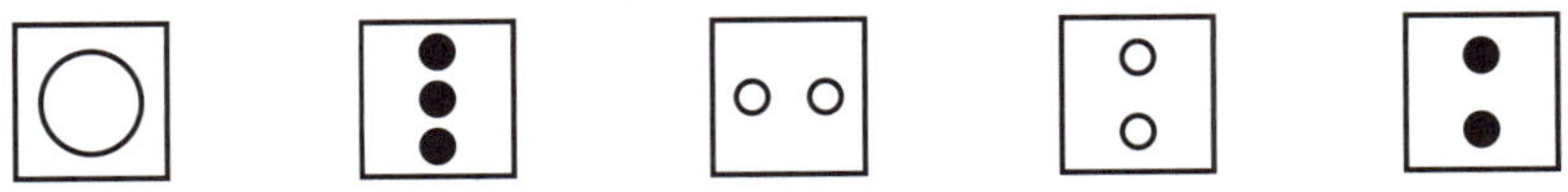

a b c d e

1

Which one completes the second pair in the same way as the first pair? Circle the letter.

11  is to  as  is to **?**

a b c d e

1

12  is to  as  is to **?**

a b c d e

1

13 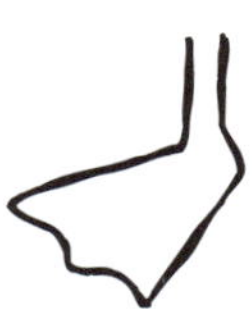 is to  as  is to **?**

a b c d e

1

Which one on the right belongs to the group on the left? Circle the letter.

14

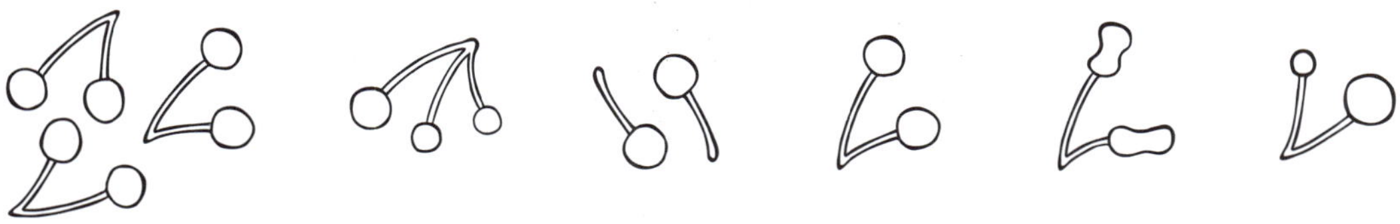

a b c d e

1

15

a b c d e

1

16

a b c d e

1

17

a b c d e

1

Which shape on the right is a reflection of the shape on the left? Circle the letter.

18

a b c d e

1

19

a b c d e

1

20

a b c d e

1

Total 20

Mixed Paper 4

In which picture on the right is the smaller picture hidden? Circle the letter.

1

a b c d e

1

2

a b c d e

1

3

a b c d e

1

Which one comes next? Circle the letter.

4

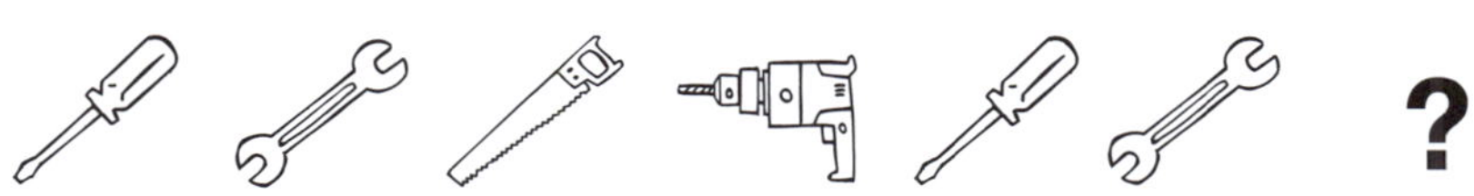

a b c d e

1

5

a b c d e

1

6

a b c d e

1

Which is the odd one out? Circle the letter.

7

a b c d e

1

8

a b c d e

1

9

a b c d e

1

10

a b c d e

1

11

a b c d e

1

12

a b c d e

1

Which one on the right completes the second pair in the same way as the first pair? Circle the letter.

13  is to  as  is to **?**

 **a**  **b**  **c**  **d**  **e**

1

14 

is to 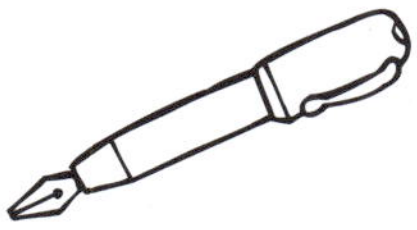 as 

is to **?**

 **a**  **b**  **c** 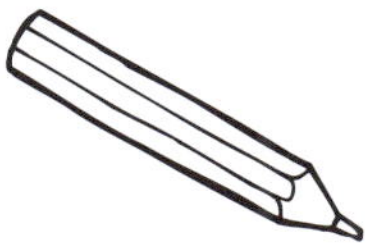 **d** 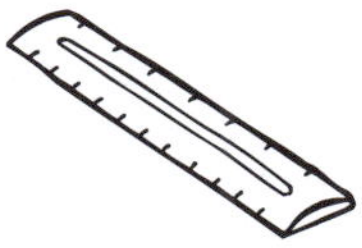 **e**

1

15 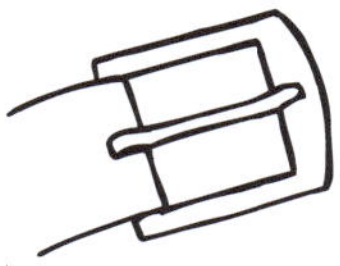 is to  as 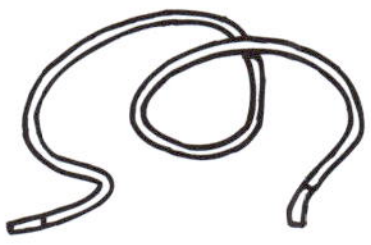 is to **?**

 **a**  **b**  **c**  **d**  **e**

1

16  is to  as  is to **?**

 **a**  **b**  **c**  **d** 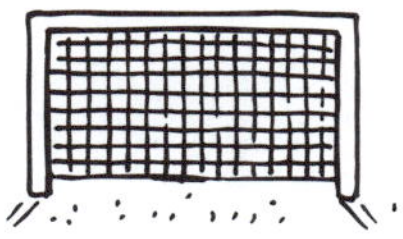 **e**

1

Which one on the right belongs to the group on the left? Circle the letter.

17

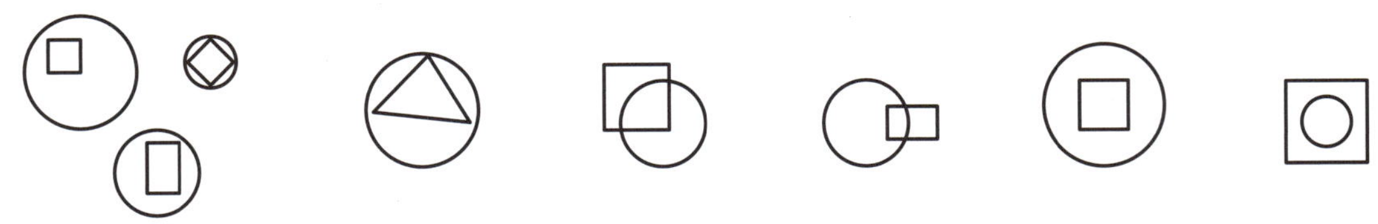

a b c d e

1

18

a b c d e

1

19

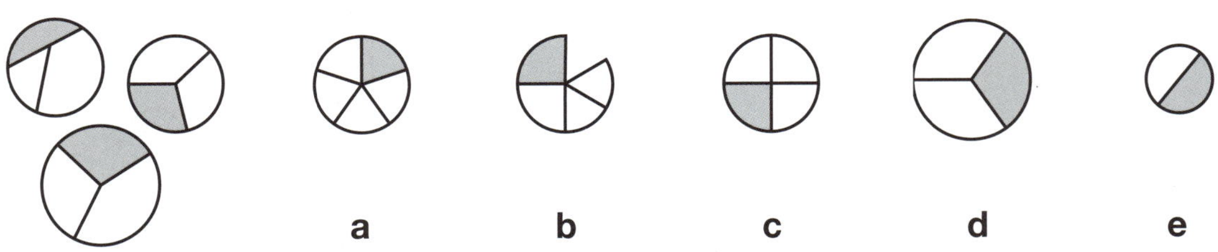

a b c d e

1

20

a b c d e

1

Total **20**

Mixed Paper 5

Which shape or picture on the right completes the second pair in the same way as the first pair? Circle the letter.

1

 is to  as 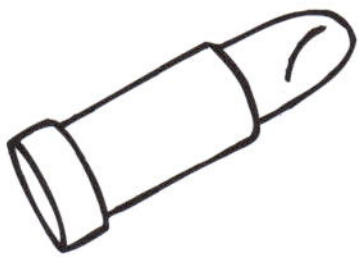 is to **?**

 **a**
 **b**
 **c**
 **d**
 **e**

1

2

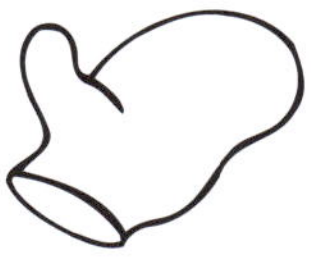 is to  as  is to **?**

 **a**
 **b**
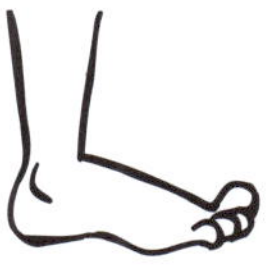 **c**
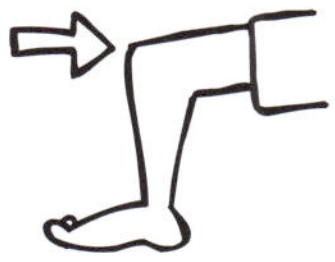 **d**
 **e**

1

3

 is to  as  is to **?**

 **a**
 **b**
 **c**
 **d**
 **e**

1

4  is to  as  is to **?**

a **b** **c** **d** **e**

1

5  is to  as 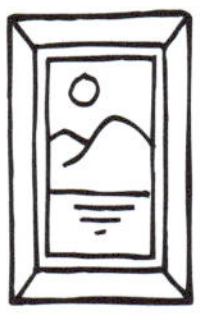 is to **?**

a **b** **c** **d** **e**

1

Which shape on the right is a reflection of the shape on the left?
Circle the letter.

6

a **b** **c** **d** **e**

1

7

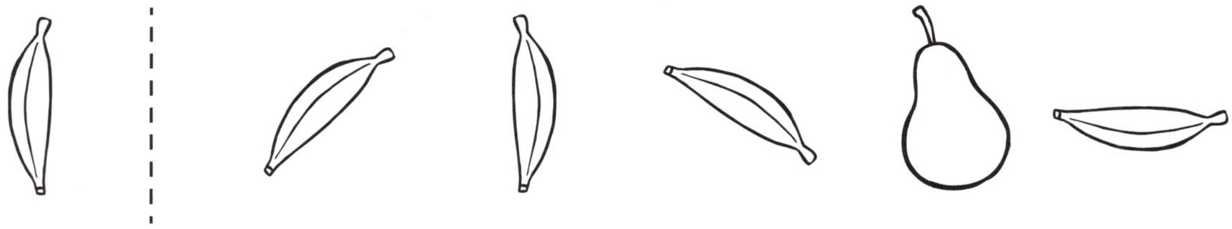

a **b** **c** **d** **e**

1

8

a **b** **c** **d** **e**

1

Which one comes next? Circle the letter.

9

a **b** **c** **d** **e**

1

10

a **b** **c** **d** **e**

1

11

a **b** **c** **d** **e**

1

Which is the odd one out? Circle the letter.

12

a **b** **c** **d** **e**

1

13

a b c d e

1

14

a b c d e

1

Which shape on the right is made up of the two shapes on the left?
Circle the letter.

15

a b c d e

1

16

a b c d e

1

17

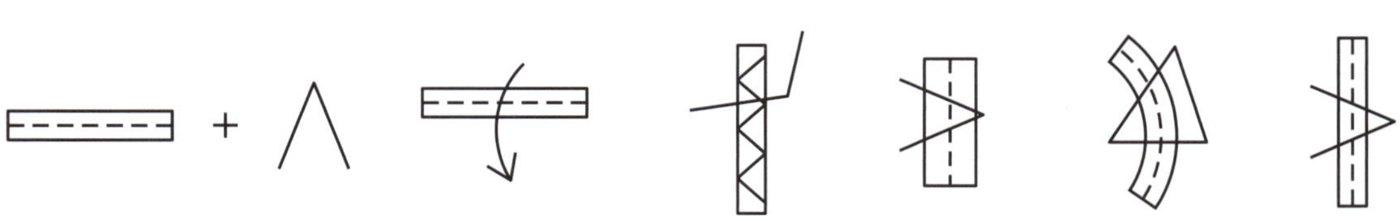

a b c d e

1

Which shape or picture on the right completes the larger square on the left? Circle the letter.

18

a b c d e

1

19

a b c d e

1

20

a b c d e

1

Total 20

Mixed Paper 6

Which picture completes the second pair in the same way as the first pair? Circle the letter.

1  is to 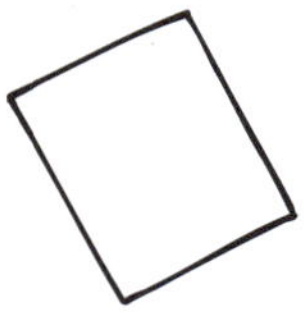 as 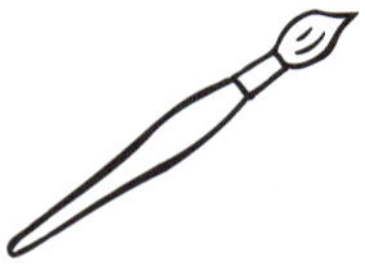 is to **?**

a

b

c

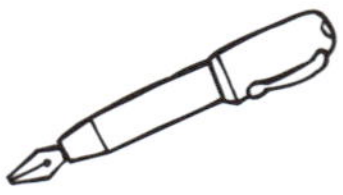
d

e

1

2 

is to  as 

is to **?**

a

b

c

d

e

1

3  is to  as  is to **?**

a

b

c

d

e

1

4  is to  as  is to **?**

a **b** **c** **d** **e**

1

Which shape on the right is made up of the two shapes on the left? Circle the letter.

5

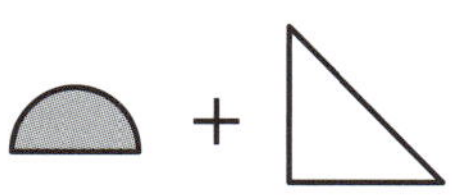

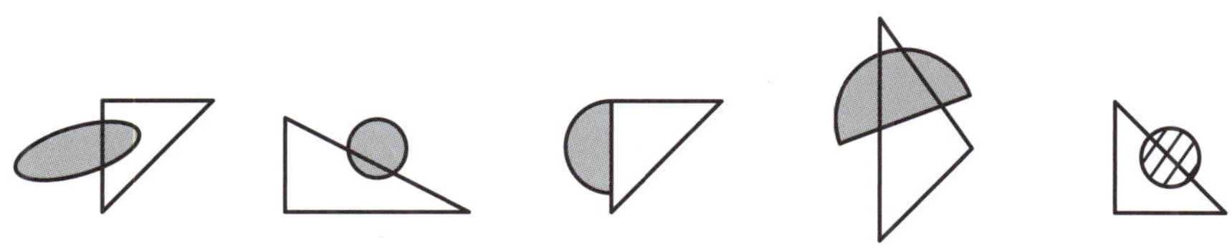

a **b** **c** **d** **e**

1

6

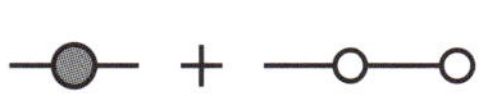

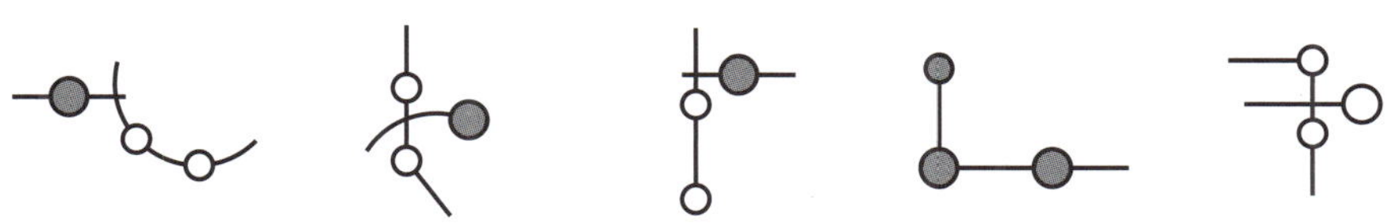

a **b** **c** **d** **e**

1

7

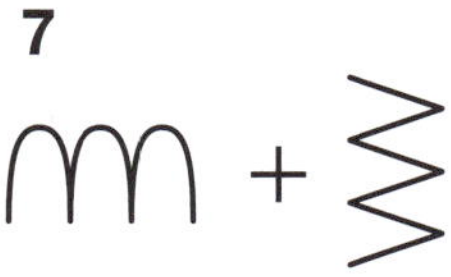

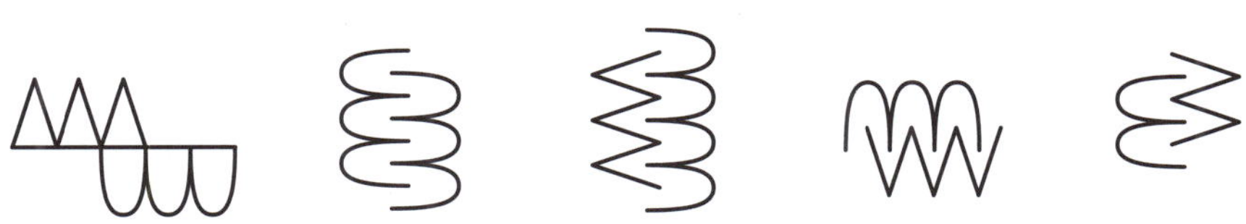

a **b** **c** **d** **e**

1

In which larger picture is the picture on the left hidden? Circle the letter.

8

a **b** **c** **d** **e**

1

9

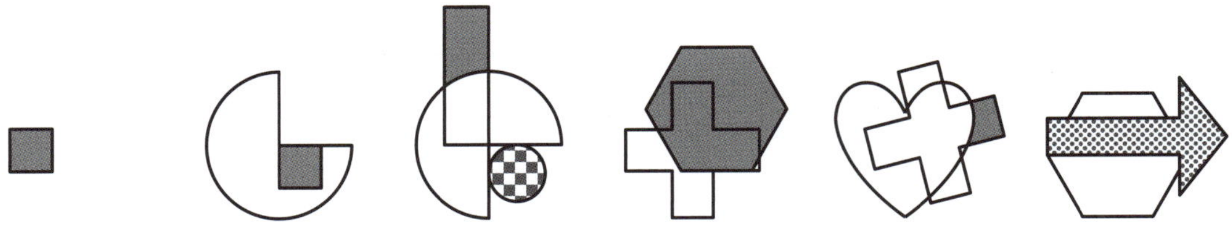

a b c d e

1

10

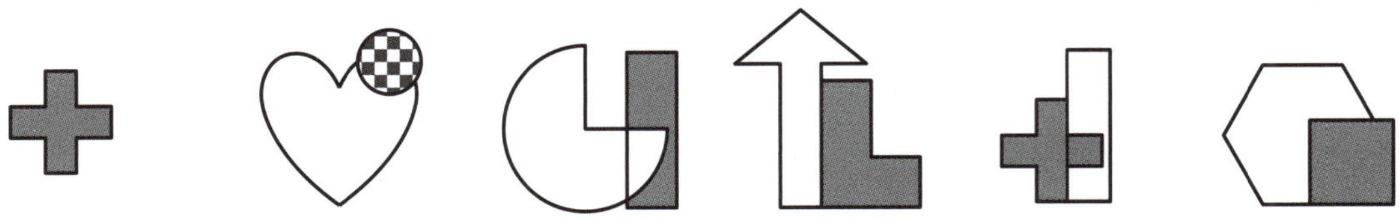

a b c d e

1

Which one comes next? Circle the letter.

11

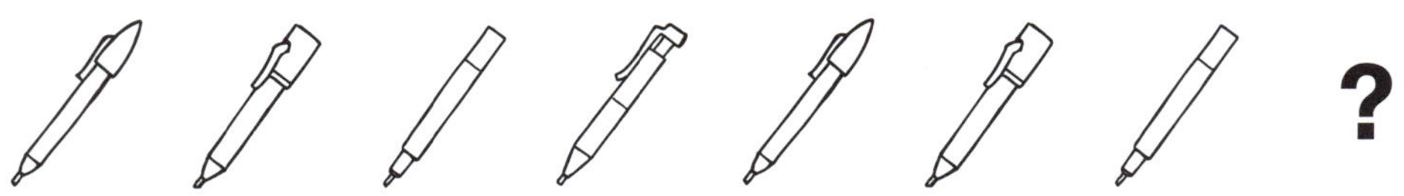

a b c d e

1

12

a b c d e

1

13

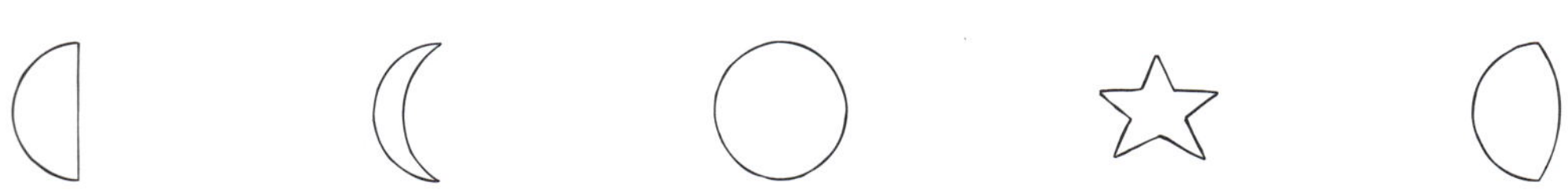

a b c d e

1

14

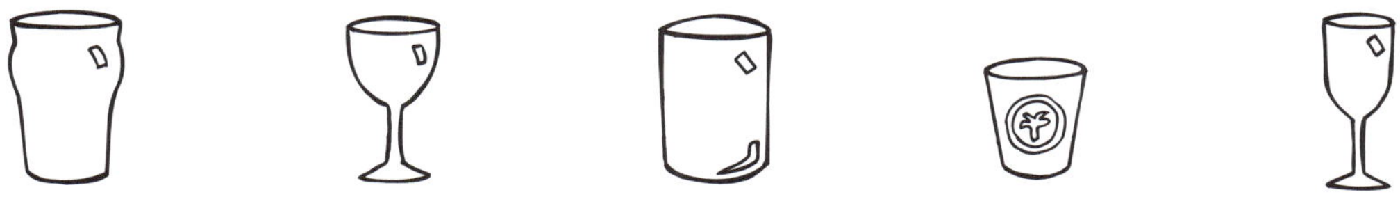

a **b** **c** **d** **e**

1

15

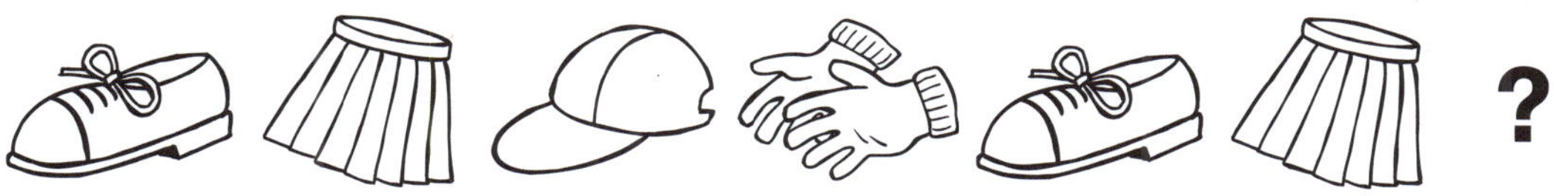

a **b** **c** **d** **e**

1

16

a **b** **c** **d** **e**

1

Which is the odd one out? Circle the letter.

17

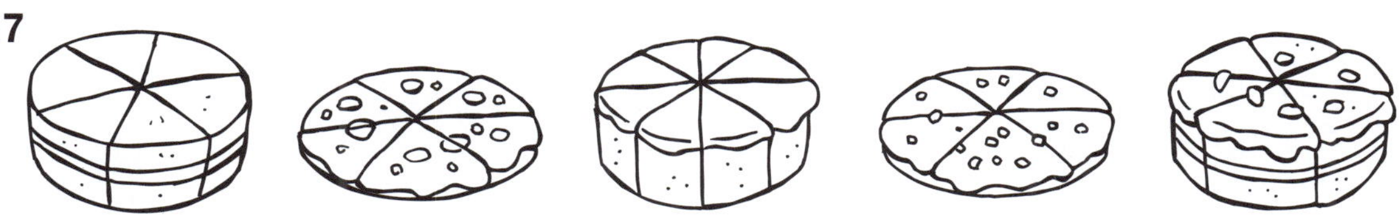

a **b** **c** **d** **e**

1

18

a b c d e

1

19

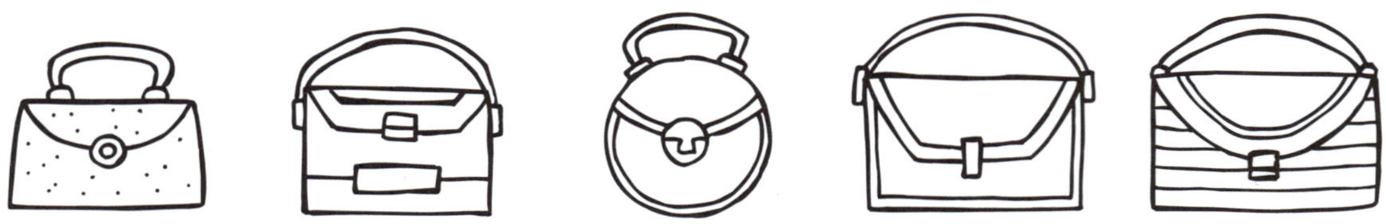

a b c d e

1

20

a b c d e

1

Total
20

Puzzle 2

Which one comes next? Circle the letter.

1

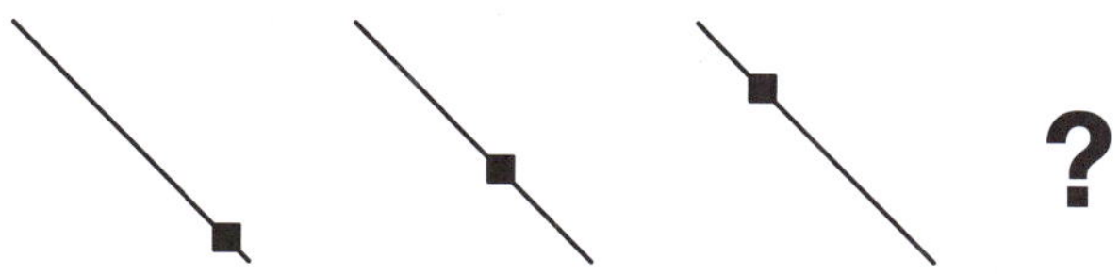

a b c d e

1

2

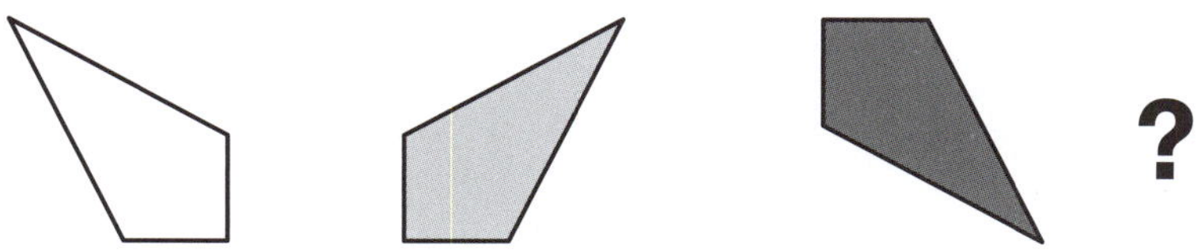

a b c d e

1

Which shape or picture completes the larger square? Circle the letter.

3

a b c d e

1

4

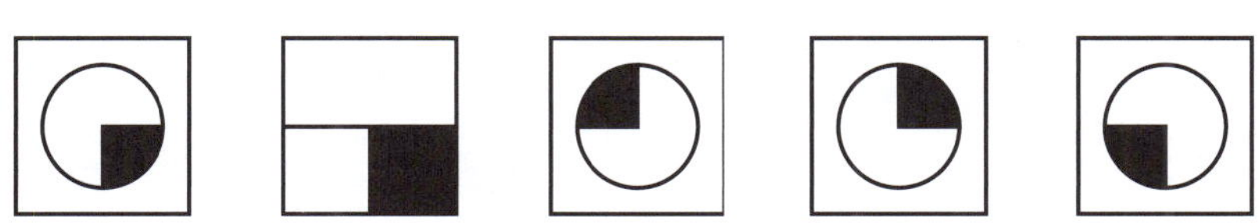

a b c d e

1

Total
4

Keywords

alternate	to come in turns, one after the other
option	something chosen or that may be chosen
reflection	the result of reflecting a shape in a given mirror line
right angle	an angle of 90° (think of the corner of a piece of paper)

Notes

Notes

Bond 11+

Non-verbal Reasoning

Ages 7–8

Assessment Practice

ANSWERS

AND PROGRESS CHART

OXFORD

Answers

Learning Paper 1: Shape
(pages 7–9)

1 **d** The arrowhead is a different shape.
2 **e** One is a square rather than a round clock.
3 **d** The flag has curved edges.
4 **d** Does not have a white square.
5 **a** The top of the gate is arched.
6 **a** The triangle has a right angle.
7 **b** The only round cushion.
8 **e** Has a black triangle rather than a square.
9 **a** The only seat that is a circle.
10 **c** The only ship, others all have wheels.
11 **d** The only triangular chocolate.
12 **b** A small cupcake rather than a large cake.

Learning Paper 2: Position
(pages 10–12)

1 **e** The black square is inside the circle.
2 **c** The shadow is on the right.
3 **b** There is a missing tooth on the bottom, not the top.
4 **b** The folded corner is top left, not bottom right.
5 **d** The black circle is not at the bottom.
6 **e** The ring is on a different finger.
7 **c** The small triangles are not at the end of the line.
8 **d** The door handle is on the left.
9 **a** The only one that has a lid.
10 **c** The shaded and black squares are opposite, not touching each other.
11 **b** The arrowhead is pointing towards the line, instead of away from it.
12 **a** The circle is not at a corner of the square.

Learning Paper 3: Angle or Rotation
(pages 13–15)

1 **b** The cross is made from diagonal lines – in all other flags, the cross is made of a horizontal and a vertical line.
2 **b** The only anticlockwise arrow.
3 **d** The only door that has one rectangular window at the top.
4 **b** All arrows except option b have a right angle.
5 **d** All figures except option d have the right 'arm' horizontal.
6 **c** All of the figures except option c are skiing diagonally.
7 **c** All of the arrows except option c are clockwise.
8 **e** All of the coils rotate clockwise except option e.
9 **e** All of the slides go clockwise around the tower except option e.
10 **d** All angles except option d are acute angles (less than a right angle).
11 **b** All the cards except option b are vertical.
12 **e** All of the shields except option e have a wider angle on the V-shape.

Learning Paper 4: Number
(pages 16–18)

1 **b** All except option b have four arrows.
2 **d** Only option d has one top panel and three lower panels.
3 **c** All stars except option c have five points.
4 **e** Has seven people rather than six.
5 **c** The coat has six buttons and the others have five.
6 **d** The picture has seven birds and the others have eight.
7 **d** The figure has two black circles and the others have one.
8 **b** The picture has four insects and the others have three.
9 **e** The shape has five sides and the others have six.
10 **a** The picture has five fish and the others have four.
11 **c** The figure has a total of five 'curves' and the others have six.
12 **d** Only option d has seven petals, the others have five or six.

Learning Papers 5–8

Learning Paper 5: Shading
(pages 19–21)

1 **d** The train has dark grey smoke coming from the chimney.
2 **d** The cat is mostly white and the others are mostly black.
3 **e** The triangle is unshaded.
4 **b** The shading is the same on the rectangle and the circle.
5 **e** The small rectangle is not black.
6 **b** Only option b has two shapes with the same shading.
7 **e** Only option e has a grey handle.
8 **e** Only option e has two squares with the same shading.
9 **c** Only option c has black at the top of the ball.
10 **d** All except option d have the overlapping section shaded black.
11 **e** Has horizontal shading lines on the 'case' for the cupcake.
12 **c** All except option c have a grey bead in the middle.

Learning Paper 6: Size (pages 22–24)

1 **e** The cross is bigger.
2 **d** This option is a branch of a tree rather than a whole tree.
3 **a** The two shapes are not the same size as each other.
4 **a** A whole car rather than parts of a car.
5 **c** The square is bigger.
6 **d** The square is bigger than the circle.
7 **b** The arrow is narrower.
8 **c** A twig rather than a larger log.
9 **e** The square inside the shape is larger.
10 **d** The black circle is smaller.
11 **b** The tent is a different shape to the others.
12 **e** This is a ladle – the rest are spoons.

Learning Paper 7: Similarities
(pages 25–27)

1 **c** All single balloons with one curved string and a balloon knot.
2 **d** All of the shapes have one half shaded.
3 **e** All single arrows with a plain V-shaped point at one end.
4 **d** All made up of three circles inside each other.
5 **e** All are hats.
6 **c** All are quadrilaterals (four-sided shapes).
7 **e** All made up of two lines at right angles to each other.
8 **d** All are single candles with a single lit flame.
9 **d** All are leaves.
10 **c** All are triangles with a small grey quadrilateral inside.
11 **e** All are snakes with simple stripes and a forked tongue.
12 **c** All are cuboids.

Learning Paper 8: Analogies or Pairing Up (pages 28–31)

1 **a** Changes from six people to two people.
2 **a** Gloves go with hat, as t-shirt goes with shorts.
3 **b** A bird flies like a plane and a fish moves in water like a submarine.
4 **d** The second picture shows the first picture upright (the object has been rotated through 90 degrees).
5 **b** The flowers in the first picture are shaded in the second picture.
6 **d** The cube in the first picture becomes a pyramid shape in the second picture.
7 **a** The first picture shows a young animal, and the second picture shows the adult animal that it grows into.
8 **d** The first picture is five of the same animal and the second picture is eight of the same animal.
9 **c** The second picture shows the transport that goes on the first picture.
10 **a** The same colour and shape on the second card with the number increased by two.
11 **e** The object is the same with plain shading changed to spotty shading.
12 **e** The container changes from a cylinder to a cuboid.

Learning Paper 9: Reflections
(pages 32–35)

1 **d** Check the position of the curved balloon.
2 **a** Count the number of wheels.
3 **c** Check each arm position.
4 **e** The handle reflects to the right.
5 **c** Check each clock.
6 **d** The string reflects to the left. Also check the pattern.
7 **e** The sun reflects to the left.
8 **b** Pay attention to the order of the people and the objects they are holding.
9 **c** Check the top of the tree and the position of the decorations.
10 **a** Check for the correct shape.
11 **d** Only $\frac{3}{4}$ moon.
12 **c** The flower is near the mirror line on the snowman with hair.

Learning Paper 10: Grids (pages 36–38)

1**a** The objects in each square in the column stay the same. The number of objects goes 3-2-1 down each column.
2 **e** The whole grid forms a symmetrical pattern.
3 **c** The objects in each square in the row stay the same. The number of objects goes 3-2-1 across each row.
4 **b** The small squares are the same colour within each column. The small squares are in the same position within the grid squares along each row.
5 **a** Each square alternates between black and grey cat – going along each row and down each column. The cat does not change except for colour.
6 **d** The arrows in each column are the same colour. The arrows along a row all point in the same direction.
7 **b** Each row and column has one of each version of the shading.
8 **d** The corner image is rotated 90 degrees clockwise around the corners of the grid.
9 **a** Both the left and right columns have the larger dogs.
10 **b** The middle column has the dark grey cat, and the bottom row has the cats the correct way up.
11 **d** Each object appears once in each column and row.
12 **a** The pictures in each column are all the same, but going down the column they are rotated by 90 degrees anticlockwise.

Learning Paper 11: Sequences
(pages 39–43)

1 **b** A repeating pattern of four animals – elephant-lion-hyena-bull. So the next animal in the sequence is the hyena.
2 **d** A repeating pattern of four animals – cow-sheep-goat-horse. So the next animal in the sequence is the horse.
3 **b** A repeating pattern of four fruits – apple-orange-banana-pear. So the next fruit in the sequence is a banana.
4 **c** A repeating pattern of four seats – bench-armchair-recliner-chair. So the next seat in the sequence is the recliner.
5 **e** A repeating pattern of four cakes so the third cake in the sequence comes next.
6 **d** A repeating pattern of three bowls so the third bowl in the sequence comes next.
7 **b** One more duck gets into the water along the sequence.
8 **e** The number of apples falling off the tree increases by one each time.
9 **e** As the plant grows the number of leaves increases but it gets to four leaves before nine leaves.
10 **c** Having wrapped a present, the next step is giving it to someone.
11 **b** The next step to building a snowman is to put the head onto the body.
12 **e** Having done the edge of a puzzle, the next step is to start filling it in.

Learning Paper 12: Hidden Shapes and Combining Shapes (pages 44–47)

1 **e**

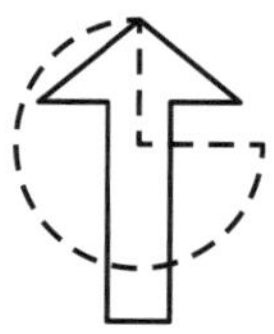

2 **b** Has the correct (matching) clock.
3 **b** Has the correct (matching) window on the house.
4 **a** It is the duck's bill.
5 **d** It is the horn on the rhino.
6 **b** It is the button on the jacket.
7 **a**

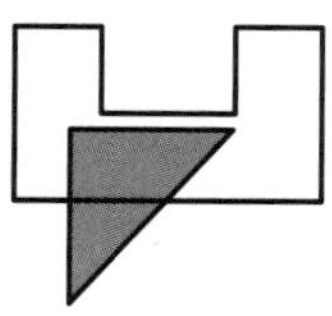

8 **b**

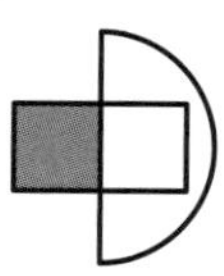

9 **e**

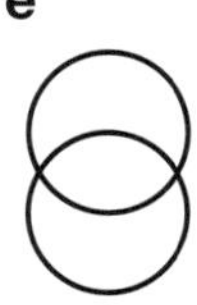

10 **d** Has a black cat with the same shape ball of wool.

11 **e**

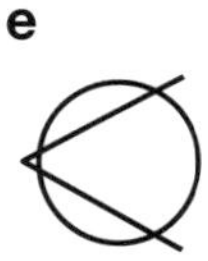

12 **e**

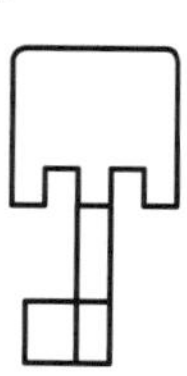

Puzzle 1 (page 48)

1 **b** This is a three repeat. The flag is laying down with the black tip and it is not a reflection.
2 **a** This is a four repeat. The bottle points to the right, the label has not been altered.
3 **c** The arm will point up to the left and the black triangle will point to the top right.
4 **c** The black square is on the middle left. The striped square is on the bottom with the stripes going from top right to bottom left.

Mixed Paper 1 (pages 49–53)

1 **e** All except option e are found in the kitchen.
2 **d** All except option d have the smoke going up vertically.
3 **e** All except option e are to do with vision and looking not sound.
4 **a** All except option a have four castles with flags.
5 **c** All the pictures on the left are wrapped sweets.
6 **d** All the shapes on the left are divided into three parts.
7 **e** All the arrows on the left have an arrowhead at each end.
8 **d** The second picture shows what you can use to protect yourself against the weather shown in the first picture.
9 **e** The second picture shows where the object in the first picture is kept.
10 **a** The second picture has the object in the first picture lying on the ground.
11 **d** The first pair of letters are put in reverse order for the second part.
12 **a** The brush in the first picture is used for the part of the body shown in the second picture.
13 **e** The second picture shows the object in the first picture turned upside down.
14 **b** The second picture is a small version of the vehicle shown in the first picture.
15 **a** Check for the correct people.
16 **d** Check each bird one at a time.

17 **b** Check each piece of cutlery one at a time.
18 **e** The sequence repeats every third image.
19 **a** The sequence repeats every fourth image.
20 **b** Another person has got onto the bus.

Mixed Paper 2 (pages 54–57)

1 **e** Check the type of chair.
2 **c** At the tip of the pen.
3 **e** Check for the correct doorhandle.
4 **c** The sequence repeats every third image so the third dog is the next one in the sequence.
5 **b** The sequence repeats every fourth image so the fourth flower is the next one in the sequence.
6 **c** The size of the fruits decreases along the sequence.
7 **b** All the flags except option b are held forming a right angle.
8 **b** All except option b have the fork on the left.
9 **a** All of the cars except option a have the steering wheel on the left.
10 **b** All of the candles except option b are cylindrical.
11 **e** Option e is the only one with straight edges on the side of the bottle.
12 **e** The A (ace) goes to the J (jack) of the same colour and shape.
13 **d** The white arrow goes to a black arrow pointing in the same direction with a line across the sign.
14 **b** The figure in the first picture is upside down in the second picture.
15 **e**

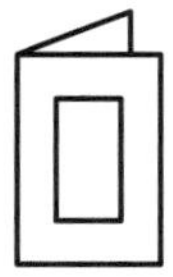

16 **a**

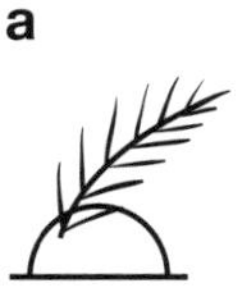

17 **c**

18 **d** The three animals in the top row go down to two in the bottom row.
19 **b** The top image is the bottom image rotated 90 degrees anti-clockwise.
20 **d** The bottom row is a reflection of the top row.

Mixed Paper 3 (pages 58–62)

1 **c** The sequence repeats every third image, so the third gate comes next.
2 **c** The sequence repeats every fourth image and the third house comes next.
3 **b** The cats are getting lighter along the sequence, with solid colour body.
4 **b** The sequence repeats every fourth image, with the fourth sign coming next.
5 **d** The sequence shows a sports team arriving at a match – so the next picture should show the match starting.
6 **b** There is an increasing number of wheels along the sequence.
7 **c** This boat is at a different angle to the others.
8 **b** The other options are all tools that would be used outdoors.
9 **d** The shapes are identical in each column.
10 **e** Each row of the grid is the same.
11 **d** The second picture shows how the animal in the first picture is transported.
12 **e** The second picture shows the person who would wear the helmet shown in the first picture.
13 **e** The second picture is the animal whose foot is shown in the first picture.
14 **c** The group on the left all have two equal size 'cherries' joined together.
15 **c** The objects in the group on the left are all for sitting on.
16 **d** The shapes on the left are all triangles.
17 **e** The shapes on the left all have one plain and one dotted line parallel along their length.

18 **a** Check the order of people from the bus stop.
19 **e** Check the angle of the head of the lamp.
20 **b** Check the different waves and the level of the horizon.

Mixed Paper 4 (pages 63–66)

1 **e** The man in option e is wearing an eyepatch.
2 **b** The scene in option b contains a squirrel.
3 **e** The plane in option e has the same shaped wing.
4 **e** A repeating pattern of four objects with the third object coming next.
5 **d** A repeating pattern of four objects with the third object coming next.
6 **e** Not yet added the tree to the painting.
7 **b** All of the other vehicles have four wheels.
8 **c** All of the other objects are spheres.
9 **b** All of the other bags have black straps.
10 **d** All of the other pictures are full flowerheads.
11 **d** All of the other pictures are musical instruments.
12 **c** All of the other pictures are small balloons.
13 **a** The second picture is the lid for the object in the first picture.
14 **b** The second object makes a mark using the substance shown in the first picture.
15 **b** The object shown in the first picture is used to fasten the object in the second picture.
16 **e** The second picture shows the goal net for the type of ball shown in the first picture.
17 **d** All of the shapes on the left are circles with a small four-sided shape within them.
18 **e** All of the shapes on the left are black ovals with a stem and a short diagonal tail.
19 **d** All of the circles on the left are divided into three parts with one part shaded.
20 **d** All of the objects on the left have handles and are used for drinking.

Mixed Paper 5 (pages 67–71)

1 **e** The first picture shows something that goes onto the second picture.
2 **c** The first picture shows something that goes onto the second picture.
3 **a** The second object is a larger version of the object in the first picture, but doing the same job.
4 **c** Lions are found on the land, whales are found in the sea.
5 **d** The second picture is a square version of the object shown in the first picture.
6 **e** The letters are also reflected.
7 **b** Option b is the only upright banana.
8 **e** The stripes are reflected.
9 **e** The sequence repeats every fourth image, so the third picture comes next.
10 **d** The number of spots increases by one each time.
11 **c** The washing machine is switched on.
12 **b** All the other cakes have nine candles.
13 **c** All the other figures have both flags on one side.
14 **e** All of the other pictures have the tree bigger than the bird.
15 **e**

16 **a**

17 **e**

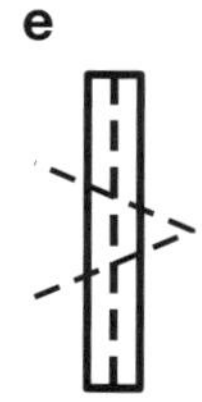

18 **c** The numbers increase going down the grid, with two animals in each square on the middle row.
19 **a** The middle row images are a reflection of those in the top row, reflected left to right.
20 **e** The bottom row is a repeat of the top row.

Mixed Paper 6 (pages 72–76)

1 **e** The first picture shows the implement used to make marks on the second picture.
2 **d** The second picture shows the item used to serve the first picture.
3 **a** The second picture shows the transport in the first picture, but outside of where it is stored.
4 **b** The second picture is a square version of the object in the first picture.
5 **c** Pay attention to the size and type of triangle and ensure the shaded shape is a semi-circle.
6 **c** Pay attention to the number of circles and the shading of them.
7 **d** Pay attention to the number of peaks on each of the shapes.
8 **b** Pay attention to the shape of the balls.
9 **a**
10 **d**
11 **c** The sequence repeats every fourth image with the fourth picture coming next.
12 **a** The number of panes increases by one each time.
13 **c** The moon is increasing in size along the sequence.
14 **a** The sequence repeats every fourth image with the third picture coming next.
15 **e** The sequence repeats every fourth image with the third picture coming next.
16 **c** The petals are falling off a flower with the number on the ground increasing along the sequence.
17 **c** All of the others have six slices.
18 **b** All of the other fires are inside within a fireplace.
19 **c** All of the other bags are rectangular in shape.
20 **d** All of the other trees are growing in the ground not a pot.

Puzzle 2 (page 77)

1 **e** The black horizontal square moves up the line. The next location is just before the top and it has not been rotated.
2 **a** The kite gets darker and turns a quarter turn clockwise each time.
3 **d** There are the same number of insects down a column, with the ones in the lower row having made a 90 degree turn clockwise compared to their direction in the row above.
4 **c** The shaded sections on the bottom are on the right and on the top on the left.

Notes

Progress Chart

Learning Papers

Shape									
									/12

Position									
									/12

Angle or Rotation									
									/12

Number									
									/12

Shading									
									/12

Size									
									/12

Similarities									
									/12

Analogies or Pairing Up									
									/12

Reflections									
									/12

Grids									
									/12

Sequences									
									/12

Hidden shapes and Combining shapes									
									/12

Mixed Papers

	1	2	3	4	5	6
1						
2						
3						
4						
5						
6						
7						
8						
9						
10						
11						
12						
13						
14						
15						
16						
17						
18						
19						
20						
	/20	/20	/20	/20	/20	/20

Puzzle 1				
				/4

Puzzle 2				
				/4